States United

Acts of Congress relating to loans and the currency

From 1842 to 1864 inclusive

States United

Acts of Congress relating to loans and the currency
From 1842 to 1864 inclusive

ISBN/EAN: 9783337232801

Printed in Europe, USA, Canada, Australia, Japan

Cover: Foto ©Suzi / pixelio.de

More available books at **www.hansebooks.com**

ACTS OF CONGRESS

RELATING TO

LOANS AND THE CURRENCY.

FROM 1842 TO 1864 INCLUSIVE.

NEW YORK:

PUBLISHED AT THE OFFICE. OF

THE BANKERS' MAGAZINE AND STATISTICAL REGISTER.

63 WILLIAM STREET, CORNER OF CEDAR STREET.

1864.

Price, One Dollar

LAWS OF THE UNITED STATES

AUTHORIZING ISSUES OF

BONDS AND TREASURY-NOTES, &c

CONTENTS.

LAWS OF THE UNITED STATES

AUTHORIZING ISSUES OF

BONDS AND TREASURY-NOTES,

&c.

CHAP. III. — AN ACT AUTHORIZING A LOAN NOT EXCEED-
ING THE SUM OF TWELVE MILLIONS OF DOLLARS.

July 21, 1841.

Vol. V. p. 438.

*Be it enacted by the Senate and House of Representatives
of the United States of America in Congress assembled,*
That the President of the United States is hereby author- *President author-ized to borrow $12,000,000 at 6 per cent.*
ized, at any time within one year from the passage of this
act, to borrow, on the credit of the United States, a sum
not exceeding twelve millions of dollars, or so much
thereof as in his opinion the exigencies of the government
may require, at a rate of interest, payable quarterly or
semiannually, not exceeding six per centum per annum,
which loan shall be made reimbursable either at the will *When reimbursable.*
of the Secretary of the Treasury, after six months' notice,
or at any time after three years from the first day of Jan-
uary next; and said money so borrowed shall be applied, *The money borrowed how to be applied.*
in addition to the money now in the Treasury, or which
may be received therein from other sources, to the payment and redemption of the Treasury-notes heretofore
authorized, which are or may be outstanding and unpaid,
and to defray any of the public expenses which have been
heretofore or which may be authorized by law, which stock *Stock how transferable.*
shall be transferable only on the books of the Treasury.

SEC. 2. *And be it further enacted,* That the Secretary *Certificates of stock to be prepared and sold.*
of the Treasury be, and he is hereby, authorized, with the
consent of the President, to cause to be prepared certificates of stock, signed by the Secretary and countersigned
by the Register of the Treasury, for the sum to be
borrowed, or any part thereof, bearing an interest not ex-

ceeding six per centum per annum, and transferable and reimbursable as aforesaid, and to cause the said certifi-

Proviso.   cates of stock to be sold : *Provided,* That no stock be sold below par.

Secretary of the Treasury to receive proposals for the loan, or, &c.   SEC. 3. *And be it further enacted,* That the Secretary of the Treasury be, and he is hereby, authorized to receive proposals for taking the said loan, or to employ an agent or agents for the purpose of negotiating the same, and to pay to him or them a reasonable commission, not exceeding one tenth of one per cent on the amount so negotiated, which sum to be allowed to such agent or agents, and such expense as may be necessarily incurred in printing and

Expenses incident to this act limited.   issuing certificates of stock, and other expenses incident to the due execution of this act, in all not exceeding twelve thousand dollars, which sum is hereby appropriated for that purpose, and shall be paid out of any money in the Treasury not otherwise appropriated.

Secretary of the Treasury authorized to purchase stock prior to time of redemption.   SEC. 4. *And be it further enacted,* That the Secretary of the Treasury is hereby authorized to purchase, at any time before the period herein limited for the redemption of stock hereby authorized, such portion thereof as the funds of the government may admit of, after meeting all

Appropriation therefor.   the demands on the Treasury, and any surplus in the Treasury is hereby appropriated to that object.

Faith of United States pledged for punctual payment of interest, &c.   SEC. 5. *And be it further enacted,* That the faith of the United States be, and is hereby, pledged for the punctual payment of the interest and redemption of said stock.

Approved July 21, 1841.

April 15, 1842.
Vol. V. p. 473.

CHAP. XXVI. — AN ACT FOR THE EXTENSION OF THE LOAN OF EIGHTEEN HUNDRED AND FORTY-ONE, AND FOR AN ADDITION OF FIVE MILLIONS OF DOLLARS THERETO, AND FOR ALLOWING INTEREST ON TREASURY-NOTES DUE.

Be it enacted by the Senate and House of Representatives of the United States of America in Congress assembled,

Time for obtaining the loan extended.   That the time limited by the first section of the act of Congress entitled " An Act authorizing a loan not exceeding the sum of twelve millions of dollars," approved

July twenty-first, eighteen hundred and forty-one, for obtaining said loan, shall be, and the same is hereby, extended for one year from the passage of this act.

SEC. 2. *And be it further enacted*, That so much of said loan as may be obtained after the passage of this act shall be made reimbursable, as shall be agreed upon and determined at the time of issuing said stock, either at the will of the Secretary of the Treasury, after six months' notice, or at any time not exceeding twenty years from the first day of January next.

SEC. 3. *And be it further enacted*, That the certificates hereafter to be issued for said loan may, when required, be in such form as shall be prescribed by the Secretary of the Treasury, so that the stock may be transferable by de- livery of the certificate, instead of being assignable on the books of the Treasury.

SEC. 4. *And be it further enacted*, That the Secretary of the Treasury be, and he hereby is, authorized to dispose of the stock hereafter to be issued, or any part thereof, at its par value, but no part thereof shall be disposed of under par until the same has been advertised a reasonable time, and proposals for subscription to said loan invited. And the said Secretary is hereby authorized to accept such proposals, if he deem it for the interest of the United States so to do, as shall offer the highest price for said stock or any part thereof; or to appoint an agent or agents, as provided in the third section of the act approved July twenty-first, eighteen hundred and forty-one, before recited, to negotiate the same : *Provided*, That no stocks shall be disposed of at a lower rate than the highest price offered in said proposals.

SEC. 5. *And be it further enacted*, That the moneys arising from duties on goods, wares, and merchandise which may be imported into the United States, or so much thereof as shall be equal to the payment, from time to time, of the interest, and to the ultimate redemption of the principal of the said stock, be, and the same are hereby, pledged for the payment and redemption of the stock hereafter to be issued under and by virtue of this act and the said act of July twenty-first, eighteen hundred and forty-one, hereby amended; and so much thereof as may be

A *

necessary to pay the interest on said stock, and redeem the same when due, is hereby appropriated to that object, to be first applied by the Secretary of the Treasury to such payments and redemption.

SEC. 6. *And be it further enacted,* That it shall be the duty of the Secretary of the Treasury to report to Congress, at the commencement of the next session, the amount of money borrowed under this act and the act hereby amended, and of whom and upon what terms it shall have been obtained, with an abstract or brief statement of all the proposals submitted for the same, distinguishing between those accepted and those rejected, and a detailed statement of the expenses of making such loans.

Report to be made to Congress of the amount of money borrowed, &c.

SEC. 7. *And be it further enacted,* That all the provisions of the said act, not hereby modified or changed, shall be and remain in force, and apply to this act.

What provisions of the former act shall remain in force.

SEC. 8. *And be it further enacted,* That the President of the United States is hereby authorized to borrow an additional sum, not exceeding the sum of five millions of dollars, if in his opinion the exigencies of the government may require the same; which additional loan shall be made within the time, and according to the provisions, of said act, as modified by this.

Additional loan authorized.

SEC. 9. *And be it further enacted,* That all Treasury-notes heretofore issued under the act entitled " An Act to authorize the issuing of Treasury-notes," approved the twelfth day of October, eighteen hundred and thirty-seven, and the acts subsequent thereto, and now outstanding and unredeemed, or which may hereafter be issued under and by virtue of the same, shall, if due and unpaid before the fifth day of March, eighteen hundred and forty-two, bear interest at the rate of six per cent per annum from that day; and when they may become due hereafter, or may have become due since the said fifth day of March, eighteen hundred and forty-two, shall bear interest from the day of their so becoming due, at the rate of six per cent per annum, until they shall be respectively redeemed: *Provided,* That such interest shall cease at the expiration of sixty days' notice, to be given at any time by the Secretary of the Treasury in one or more of the principal papers published at the seat of government, of a readiness to redeem

Treasury-notes due and unpaid, &c., to bear 6 per cent interest.

Act of Oct. 12, 1837, ch. 2.

Proviso.

the same. And the said interest shall be payable semi- _{Interest payable semiannually}
annually at the Treasury of the United States, on the first
days of January and July in every year.

Approved April 15, 1842.

CHAP. LXIV. — AN ACT TO AUTHORIZE AN ISSUE OF   *July* 22, 1846.
TREASURY-NOTES AND A LOAN.   Vol. IX. p. 39.

Be it enacted by the Senate and House of Representatives of the United States of America in Congress assembled, That the President of the United States is hereby
authorized to cause Treasury-notes to be issued for such _{Issue of Treasury-notes authorized, not exceeding ten millions to be outstanding at any one time.}
sum or sums as the exigencies of the government may
require, and, in place of such of the same as may be
redeemed, to cause others to be issued ; but not exceeding
the sum of ten millions of dollars of this emission outstanding at any one time, and to be issued under limitations and other provisions contained in the act entitled
"An Act to authorize the issue of Treasury-notes," ap- _{To be issued under the limitations of the act of 1837, ch. 2.}
proved the twelfth of October, one thousand eight hundred
and thirty-seven, except that the authority hereby given to
issue Treasury-notes shall expire at the end of one year
from the passage of this act.

SEC. 2. *And be it further enacted,* That the President,
if in his opinion it shall be the interest of the United
States so to do, instead of issuing the whole amount of
Treasury-notes authorized by the first section of this act,
may borrow on the credit of the United States such an _{The President may borrow money in lieu of issuing Treasury-notes, and issue stock for the sum borrowed, &c.}
amount of money as he may deem proper, and issue therefor stock of the United States for the sum thus borrowed,
in the same form, and under the same restrictions, limitations, and provisions, as are contained in the act of Congress approved April fifteenth, one thousand eight hundred
and forty-two, entitled "An act for the extension of the
loan of eighteen hundred and forty-one, and for an addition of five millions of dollars thereto, and for allowing _{1842, ch. 26.}
interest on Treasury-notes due" : *Provided, however,*
That the sum so borrowed, together with the Treasury- _{Whole amount not to exceed $10,000,000.}
notes issued by the virtue of this act, shall not, in the

whole, exceed the sum of ten millions of dollars : *And*

No commission
to be allowed. *provided, further,* That no commission shall be allowed or paid for the negotiation of the loan authorized by this act, and also that the said stock shall be redeemable at a period not longer than ten years from issue thereof.

Not to bear a
higher rate of in-
terest than 6 per
cent. Sec. 3. *And be it further enacted,* That the Treasury-notes and the stock issued under the provisions of this act shall not bear a higher rate of interest than six per centum per annum, and no part thereof shall be disposed of at less than par.

No compensation
to be made to any
salaried officer for
preparing, signing,
and issuing said
notes, &c. Sec. 4. *And be it further enacted,* That no compensation shall be made to any officer, whose salary is fixed by law, for preparing, signing, or issuing Treasury-notes; nor shall any clerks be employed beyond the number authorized by the act herein referred to.

Sec. 5. *And be it further enacted,* That the sum of $ 50,000 appro-
priated for paying
the amount of
certain purloined
Treasury-notes. fifty thousand dollars be, and the same is hereby, appropriated, out of any money in the Treasury not otherwise appropriated, for the purpose of paying the amount of certain Treasury-notes (which, having been received or redeemed by any authorized officer of the government, were subsequently purloined or stolen, and put into circulation without evidence on their face of their having been See act of Aug.
10, 1846, ch. 180. cancelled) to the respective holders, who may have received the same, or any of them, for a full consideration, in the usual course of business, without notice or knowledge of the same having been stolen, or cancelled, or altered, and without any circumstances to cast suspicion on the good faith or due caution with which they may have received the same.

Approved July 22, 1846.

August 6, 1846.
Vol. IX. p. 64. CHAP. XC. — INDEPENDENT TREASURY ACT.

On and after Jan.
1, 1847, the duties,
taxes, &c. accruing
to the United States
shall be paid in
gold and silver coin
or in Treasury-
notes. Sec. 18. *And be it further enacted,* That on the first day of January, in the year one thousand eight hundred and forty-seven, and thereafter, all duties, taxes, sales of public lands, debts, and sums of money accruing or becoming due to the United States, and also all sums due, for postages or otherwise, to the general post-office department, shall be paid in gold and silver coin only, or in Treasury-notes issued under the authority of the United States: *Provided,* That the Secretary of the Treasury shall publish monthly, in two newspapers at the city of _{Monthly publication.} Washington, the amount of specie at the several places of deposit, the amount of Treasury-notes or drafts issued, and the amount outstanding on the last day of each month.

SEC. 19. *And be it further enacted,* That on the first _{On and after April 1, 1847, all payments to be made in gold and silver coin, or in Treasury-notes if the creditor agrees to receive them.} day of April, one thousand eight hundred and forty-seven, and thereafter, every officer or agent engaged in making disbursements on account of the United States, or of the general post-office, shall make all payments in gold and silver coin, or in Treasury-notes, if the creditor agree to receive said notes in payment; and any receiving or disbursing officer or agent who shall neglect, evade, or violate _{Violation of this and the preceding section to be reported to the President and to Congress.} the provisions of this and the last preceding section of this act, shall, by the Secretary of the Treasury, be immediately reported to the President of the United States, with the facts of such neglect, evasion, or violation, and also to Congress, if in session; and if not in session, at the commencement of its session next after the violation takes place.

CHAP. CLXXX. — AN ACT TO PROVIDE FOR THE PAY- _{August 10, 1846.} MENT OF THE EVIDENCES OF PUBLIC DEBT IN CERTAIN _{Vol. IX. p. 106.} CASES.

Be it enacted by the Senate and House of Representa lives of the United States of America in Congress assembled, That whenever it shall appear to the satisfaction of the Secretary of the Treasury, upon proof taken in _{Secretary of the Treasury to redeem Treasury - note which has been stolen and put into circulation and not cancelled.} the manner hereinafter directed, that any Treasury-note, which has been, before the passage of this act, received or redeemed by any authorized officer of the government, has been subsequently purloined or stolen, and put into circulation without having upon it any evidence or marks _{Act of July 22 1846, see .} of having been cancelled, and has been received by any person or institution for a full consideration, in the usual

2

course of business, without notice or knowledge of the same having been redeemed or received as aforesaid, or having been cancelled, or having been purloined or stolen as aforesaid, and without any circumstances existing to create suspicion of the good faith or due caution with which the same may have been received by such person or institution, he shall be, and hereby is, authorized to cause the amount of such note to be paid to the innocent holder thereof, out of any money in the Treasury not otherwise *Proviso as to na-* appropriated. *Provided*, That the facts upon which any *ture of evidence re-* *quired to prove the* such payment shall be made shall be proved by the oath or *facts.* affirmation of a credible witness or witnesses, taken before any judge of the United States, or of the highest court of record, or of the presiding judge of any court, exercising unlimited jurisdiction in amount, of any State, Territory, or district, and of the taking of which testimony due notice shall previously be given to the district-attorney of the United States for the district in which testimony is taken, who shall be at liberty to appear and propound questions to such witnesses, all of which evidence shall be trans- mitted to the Secretary of the Treasury, and preserved in *False swearing* his department; and all wilful false swearing upon such *to be perjury.* examination shall be, and hereby is declared to be, per- jury, and liable to the punishment for that offence pre- scribed by the laws of the United States. *And provided* *Statement to be* *further*, That a statement of all Treasury-notes paid *submitted to Con-* *gress.* under the provisions of this act, within the preceding year, shall be submitted to Congress with the annual report of the Secretary of the Treasury in relation to the finances.

SEC. 2. *And be it further enacted*, That when any *Officers or agents* officer or agent of the United States, duly authorized to *of the United States* *who have or may* receive, redeem, or cancel any Treasury-notes issued by *receive such notes* *to be credited with* authority of law, has received or shall receive, or has *their amount.* paid or shall pay, any Treasury-note which has been pre- viously received or redeemed by any officer or agent hav- *Credits made to* ing authority to receive or redeem such note, and which *be sanctioned.* had subsequently thereto been purloined and put into circulation, the Secretary of the Treasury, upon full and satisfactory proof that the same has been paid upon good faith, and in the exercise of ordinary prudence, may allow a credit for the amount of such note to the officer or agent so receiving or paying the same, and all credits which have before the passage of this act been allowed in such cases, and under such circumstances, are hereby sanctioned.

SEC. 3. *And be it further enacted,* That all acts and parts of acts heretofore enacted, which are supplied by this act, so far as the same may not have been acted on, are hereby repealed; and so far as they may have been acted upon, they are ratified and confirmed.

Repeal of acts supplied by this act if not acted on; if acted on, ratified and confirmed.

Approved August 10, 1846.

CHAP. V.—AN ACT AUTHORIZING THE ISSUE OF TREASURY-NOTES, A LOAN, AND FOR OTHER PURPOSES.

Jan. 28, 1847.
Vol. IX. p. 118.

Be it enacted by the Senate and House of Representatives of the United States of America in Congress assembled, That the President of the United States is hereby authorized to cause Treasury-notes, for such sum or sums as the exigencies of the government may require, but not exceeding, in the whole amount of notes issued, the sum of twenty-three millions of dollars, and of denominations not less than fifty dollars for any one note, to be prepared, signed, and issued, in the manner hereinafter provided.

$23,000,00: of Treasury-notes authorized.

SEC. 2. *And be it further enacted,* That the said Treasury-notes authorized to be issued by the first section of this act shall be reimbursed and redeemed by the United States, at the Treasury thereof, after the expiration of one year or two years from the dates of the said notes respectively; from which said dates they shall bear such interest, until they shall be respectively redeemed, as shall be expressed upon the face of the said notes; which rate of interest upon each several issue of the said notes shall be fixed by the Secretary of the Treasury, by and with the advice and approbation of the President, but shall in no case exceed the rate of interest of six per centum per annum: *Provided,* That, after the maturity of any of the said notes, such interest shall cease at the expiration of sixty days' notice, to be given at any time by

When to be paid.

Rate of interest.

Interest to cease sixty days after notice.

the Secretary of the Treasury, in one or more of the principal papers published at the seat of government, of a readiness to redeem the same. The reimbursement herein provided for shall be made at the Treasury of the United States to the holders of the said notes respectively, upon presentment, and shall include the principal of each note, and the interest which may be due thereon at the time of payment. For this reimbursement, at the time and times herein specified, the faith of the United States is hereby solemnly pledged.

Notes how signed, &c.

SEC. 3. *And be it further enacted,* That the said Treasury-notes shall be prepared under the direction of the Secretary of the Treasury, and shall be signed, on behalf of the United States, by the Treasurer thereof, and countersigned by the Register of. the Treasury ; and that those officers respectively shall, as checks upon each other, and

Accounts to be kept.

to secure the public safety, keep separate, full, and accurate accounts of the number, date, denomination, and amount, of all the notes signed and countersigned by them respectively, which said account shall be entered in a book or books, to be provided for that purpose, and carefully preserved in the Treasury Department ; and also similar accounts, kept and preserved in the same manner, of all the said notes redeemed, as the same shall be returned and cancelled ; and the Treasurer shall further account, quarterly, for all such notes delivered to him for signature or issue by the Register. The Treasurer and Register of the Treasury are hereby authorized, by and with the consent and approbation of the Secretary of the Treasury, to em-

Additional clerks authorized.

ploy such additional temporary clerks as the duties enjoined upon them by this act may render necessary : *Provided,* Said number shall not exceed five, and with a salary of not more than at the rate of twelve hundred dollars to each per annum.

SEC. 4. *And be it further enacted,* That the Secretary of the Treasury is hereby authorized, with the approbation of the President of the United States, to cause to be issued such portion of the said Treasury-notes as the President may think expedient, in payment of debts due by the United

May be issued to creditors.

States, to such public creditors, or other persons, as may choose to receive such notes in payment, as aforesaid, at

par. And the Secretary of the Treasury is further author- May be pledged but not for less than par.
ized, with the approbation of the President of the United
States, to borrow, from time to time, such sums as the
President may think expedient, on the credit of such notes:
Provided, however, That no Treasury-notes shall be
pledged, hypothecated, sold, or disposed of in any wise for
any purpose whatever, directly or indirectly, for any sum
less than the amount of such notes, including the principal
and interest thereon when disposed of.

SEC. 5. *And be it further enacted,* That the said Treas- How transferable.
ury-notes shall be transferable, by delivery and assignment
indorsed thereon, by the person to whose order the same
shall, on the face thereof, have been made payable.

SEC. 6. *And be it further enacted,* That the said Treas- To be receivable for all public dues.
ury-notes shall be received in payment of all duties and
taxes laid by the authority of the United States, of all
public lands sold by the said authority, and of all debts to
the United States of any character whatsoever, which may
be due and payable at the time when said Treasury-notes
may be so offered in payment; and on every such payment credit shall be given for the amount of the principal
and interest which, on the day of such payment, may be
due on the note or notes thus given in payment.

SEC. 7. *And be it further enacted,* That every collector, On payment a receipt to be taken,
receiver of public moneys, or other officer or agent of the
United States, shall, on the receipt of any Treasury-notes
in payment for the government, take from the holder
thereof a receipt on the back of each of said notes, stating
distinctly the date, and the amount received; and shall
keep, according to such forms as shall be prescribed by the
Secretary of the Treasury, entries of whom received, the and entry made.
number, date, and respective amounts of principal and interest of each and every Treasury-note thus received; and
on delivering the same to the Treasury shall receive credit
for the amount paid as prescribed by the last section:
Provided, no error shall appear.

SEC. 8. *And be it further enacted,* That the Secretary
of the Treasury be, and he is hereby, authorized and directed to cause to be reimbursed and paid the principal Payment.
and interest of the Treasury-notes which may be issued by
virtue of this act, at the several time and times when the

same, according to the provisions of this act, should be thus reimbursed and paid. And the Secretary is further

Purchase by United States. authorized to make purchases of the said notes at par for the amount of the principal and interest due at the time

Appropriation for payment of purchase on such notes. And so much of unappropriated money in the Treasury as may be necessary for that purpose is hereby appropriated for paying the principal and interest of said notes.

Penalty for forging or counterfeiting, &c. said notes. Sec. 9. *And be it further enacted,* That if any person shall falsely make, forge, or counterfeit, or cause or procure to be falsely made, forged, or counterfeited, or willingly aid or assist in falsely making, forging, or counterfeiting, any note in imitation of, or purporting to be, a Treasury-note aforesaid, or shall falsely alter, or cause or procure to be falsely altered, or willingly aid or assist in falsely altering, any Treasury-note issued as aforesaid, or shall pass, utter, or publish, or attempt to pass, utter, or publish as true, any false, forged, or counterfeited note, purporting to be a Treasury-note as aforesaid, knowing the same to be falsely forged or counterfeited, or shall pass, utter, or publish as true, any falsely altered Treasury-note issued as aforesaid, knowing the same to be falsely altered, every such person shall be deemed and adjudged guilty of felony, and, being thereof convicted by due course of law, shall be sentenced to be imprisoned and kept to hard labor for a period not less than three years nor more than ten years, and to be fined in a sum not exceeding five thousand dollars.

Penalty for making or keeping an engraved plate, &c. of said notes. Sec. 10. *And be it further enacted,* That if any person shall make or engrave, or cause or procure to be made or engraved, or shall have in his custody or possession, any metallic plate engraved after the similitude of any plate from which any notes issued as aforesaid shall have been printed, with intent to use such plate, or cause or suffer the same to be used in forging or counterfeiting any of the notes issued as aforesaid, or shall have in his custody or possession any blank note or notes, engraved and printed after the similitude of any notes issued as aforesaid, with intent to use such blanks, or cause or suffer the same to be used in forging or counterfeiting any of the notes issued as aforesaid, or shall have in his custody or possession any paper adapted to the making of notes, and similar to the paper upon which any such notes shall have been issued, with intent to use such paper or cause or suffer the same to be used in forging or counterfeiting any of the notes issued as aforesaid, every such person, being thereof convicted by due course of law, shall be sentenced to be imprisoned and kept to hard labor for a term not less than three nor more than ten years, and fined in a sum not exceeding five thousand dollars.

SEC. 11. *And be it further enacted,* That the Secretary of the Treasury be, and he is hereby, authorized to make and issue, from time to time, such instructions, rules, and regulations to the several collectors, receivers of public money, depositaries, and all others who may be authorized to receive the said Treasury-notes on behalf of, and as agents in any capacity for, the United States, as to the safe-keeping, disposition, return, and cancelling of the said notes so paid to and received by them, respectively, and as to their accounts and returns to the Department of such receipts as may seem to him best calculated to promote the public interest and convenience, and secure the United States and the holders of the notes against fraud and losses.

Secretary of the Treasury to make rules, &c.

SEC. 12. *And be it further enacted,* That, in lieu of the notes authorized by this act which may be redeemed, other notes may be issued : *Provided, however,* The amount of such notes outstanding, together with the stock issued by virtue of the thirteenth and sixteenth sections of this act, shall not exceed the sum of twenty-three millions of dollars.

Reissue.

Amount not to exceed $23,000,000.

SEC. 13. *And be it further enacted,* That it shall be lawful for the holders of the aforesaid Treasury-notes to present them, at any time, to the Treasury of the United States, or to any Assistant Treasurer, or to such collectors of the customs and receivers of public moneys as may be designated by the Secretary of the Treasury ; and the holders of the said Treasury-notes shall be entitled to receive therefor the amount of the principal of the said notes in a certificate or certificates of funded stock, bearing interest at six per centum per annum from the date of such presentment of said Treasury-notes, and for the interest

May be converted into stock.

shall be paid in money; and the stock thus to be issued shall be transferable on the books of the Treasury : *Provided, however, and be it further enacted,* That it shall be lawful for the United States to reimburse the stock thus created at any time after the last day of December, one thousand eight hundred and sixty-seven.

Stock when reimbursable.

Same subject. SEC. 14. *And be it further enacted,* That it shall and may be lawful for the holder of any Treasury-notes issued, or authorized to be issued, under this act, or any laws heretofore passed, to convert the same into certificates of funded stock, upon the same terms and in the same manner hereinbefore provided in relation to the Treasury-notes authorized by the first section of this act.

Act of 1846, ch. 14, extended. SEC. 15. *And be it further enacted,* That the authority to issue Treasury-notes authorized by the " Act authorizing an issue of Treasury-notes and a loan," approved July twenty-second, one thousand eight hundred and forty-six, be, and the same is hereby, extended to the same period fixed for the Treasury-notes authorized by this act, and upon the same terms and conditions herein specified : *Provided,* That the Treasury-notes authorized by this section shall not exceed five millions of dollars.

Stock may be issued instead of notes. SEC. 16. *And be it further enacted,* That the President, if in his opinion it shall be the interest of the United States so to do, instead of issuing the whole amount of Treasury-notes authorized by the first section of this act, may borrow, on the credit of the United States, such an amount of money as he may deem proper, and issue therefor stock of the United States, bearing interest at a rate not exceeding six per centum per annum for the sum thus borrowed, redeemable after thirty-first December, eighteen hundred and sixty-seven : *Provided, however,* That the sum so borrowed, together with the Treasury-notes issued under the first and twelfth sections of this act outstanding, and the stock created by this and the thirteenth sections of this act, shall not in the whole exceed the sum of twenty-three millions of dollars : *And provided further,* That no stocks shall be issued at a less rate than par.

Whole amount not to exceed $23,000,000.

Proviso.

Interest payable 1st of January and July. SEC. 17. *And be it further enacted,* That the interest on the stock created by this act shall be payable semiannually, on the first days of January and July in each year.

SEC. 18. *And be it further enacted,* That the certificates to be issued under this act shall be signed by the Register of the Treasury, and the Secretary of the Treasury shall cause each of said certificates to be sealed with the seal of his department.

Certificates of stock how signed.

SEC. 19. *And be it further enacted,* That, for the payment of the stock which may be created under the provisions of this act, the sales of public lands are hereby pledged, and it is hereby made the duty of the Secretary of the Treasury to use and apply all moneys which may be received into the Treasury for the sales of the public lands after the first day of January, eighteen hundred and forty-eight, first, to pay the interest on all stocks issued by virtue of this act; and, secondly, to use the balance of said receipts, after paying the interest aforesaid, in the purchase of said stocks at their market value : *Provided,* No more than par shall be paid for said stocks.

Proceeds of public lands pledged for redemption

Proviso repealed, 1849, chap. 100, sec. 3.

SEC. 20. *And be it further enacted,* That a sum not exceeding twenty thousand dollars, to be paid out of any unappropriated money in the Treasury, be, and the same is hereby, appropriated for defraying the expense of preparing, printing, engraving, and otherwise incident to the issuing of the Treasury-notes and stock authorized by this act: *Provided,* That no compensation shall be made to any officer whose salary is fixed by law, for preparing, signing, or issuing Treasury-notes or certificates of stock.

Contingent expenses.

SEC. 21. *And be it further enacted,* That it shall be, and hereby is, made the duty of the Secretary of the Treasury to cause a statement to be published monthly of the amount of all Treasury-notes issued or redeemed in pursuance of the provisions of this act; and that the power to issue Treasury-notes conferred on the President of the United States by this act shall cease and determine six months after the exchange and ratification of a treaty of peace with the Republic of Mexico.

Amount issued or redeemed to be published monthly.

Issue, when to cease.

SEC. 22. *And be it further enacted,* That it shall be the duty of the Secretary of the Treasury to report to Congress, at the commencement of each session, the amount of Treasury-notes which have been issued under the provisions of this act, the amount redeemed, and the manner in which redeemed, the amount purchased, and of whom,

Report to Congress at each session.

3   B*

and at what time purchased, and the amount reissued, stating in lieu of which redemption they are reissued, with the date of such reissue, during the preceding year.

Approved January 28, 1847.

March 31, 1848.
Vol. IX. p. 217.

CHAP. XXVI. — AN ACT TO AUTHORIZE A LOAN NOT TO EXCEED THE SUM OF SIXTEEN MILLIONS OF DOLLARS.

Be it enacted by the Senate and House of Representatives of the United States of America in Congress assembled, That the President of the United States be, and he is hereby, authorized, at any time within one year from the passage of this act, to borrow, on the credit of the United States, a sum not exceeding sixteen millions of dollars, or so much thereof as in his opinion the exigencies of the government may require, at a rate of interest not exceeding six per centum per annum, payable quarterly or semi-annually, which loan shall be made reimbursable at any time after twenty years from the first day of July next after the passage of this act; and said money, so borrowed, shall, on being first duly appropriated therefor, be applied, in addition to the money now in the Treasury, or which may be received therein from other sources, to defray any of the public expenses which have been heretofore, or may be hereafter, authorized by law, and the stock issued upon such loan shall be transferable on the books of the Treasury.

Loan of 16,000,000 dollars authorized.

Interest when payable.

Stock transferable.

SEC. 2. *And be it further enacted,* That the Secretary of the Treasury be, and he is hereby, authorized, with the consent of the President of the United States, to cause to be prepared certificates of stock, which shall be signed by the Register of the Treasury and sealed with the seal of the Treasury Department, for the sum to be borrowed as aforesaid, or any part thereof, bearing an interest not to exceed six per centum per annum, and transferable and reimbursable as aforesaid, and to cause said certificates of stock to be sold : *Provided,* That no part of said stock be sold below par ; *And provided, also,* That, whenever required so to do, the Secretary of the Treasury shall cause

Certificates of stock.

How sold.

Coupons for interest.

to be attached to any certificate or certificates to be issued under this act coupons of interest; and any certificate having such coupons of interest attached to it may be transferable by delivery of the certificate, instead of being assignable on the books of the Treasury; but no certificate of stock shall be issued for a less amount than fifty dollars.

Certificates transferable by delivery.

SEC. 3. *And be it further enacted*, That the Secretary of the Treasury be, and he is hereby, authorized to receive proposals for the taking of such loan, or any part or parts thereof; and that, before disposing of the said stock issued for such loan, the Secretary of the Treasury shall cause to be inserted in one or two public newspapers printed in the city of Washington, and in one or two public newspapers printed in the principal city or capital of each State, an advertisement stating that bids and proposals for such loan will be received until a certain day, to be specified in such advertisement, not more than sixty days or less than twenty days from the time of the first insertion of said advertisement in one or two newspapers in the city of Washington, and stating the amount of the loan required, and in what instalments, and when and where it will be required to be paid. And all such proposals shall be required to be sealed, and shall be opened by the Secretary, or other officer of the department, on the day appointed, publicly, and in the presence of such persons as may choose to attend; and no proposals shall be withdrawn after the same shall have been received at the Treasury Department; and the said Secretary may pay such expenses as may be necessarily incurred in printing and issuing certificates of stock: *Provided, however*, That the employment of agents, and other expenses incident to the execution of this act, shall not in all exceed the sum of sixteen thousand dollars, which sum of sixteen thousand dollars is hereby appropriated for these purposes, and shall be paid out of any money in the Treasury not otherwise appropriated; *And provided*, That no compensation shall be allowed to any officer whose salary is fixed by law, for any service performed by him in the execution of this act.

Proposals for the loan may be invited.

Contingent expenses of this loan.

Proviso.

SEC. 4. *And be it further enacted*, That the faith of the

The public faith pledged for redemption. United States is hereby pledged to provide and establish sufficient revenues for the regular payment of the interest, and for the redemption of said stock. And the principal sum borrowed under the provisions of this act, and the interest thereon, as the same shall, from time to time, become due and payable, shall be paid out of any money in the Treasury not otherwise appropriated.

Appropriation.

Purchase of stock when there are surplus funds in the Treasury.

SEC. 5. *And be it further enacted,* That the Secretary of the Treasury be, and he is hereby, authorized to purchase, at any time before the period herein limited for the redemption of the stock hereby created, such portion thereof at the market price, not below par, as the funds of the government may admit of, after meeting all the demands on the Treasury ; and any surplus that hereafter may be in the Treasury is hereby appropriated to that object.

Report to be made of things done under this act.

SEC. 6. *And be it further enacted,* That it shall be the duty of the Secretary of the Treasury to report to Congress, at the commencement of the next session, the amount of money borrowed under this act, and of whom, and on what terms, it shall have been obtained, with an abstract or brief statement of all the proposals submitted for the same, distinguishing between those accepted and those rejected, with a detailed statement of the expenses of making such loans.

Approved March 31, 1848.

March 3, 1849.
Vol. IX. p. 369.

CHAP. C. — AN ACT MAKING APPROPRIATIONS FOR THE CIVIL AND DIPLOMATIC EXPENSES OF GOVERNMENT FOR THE YEAR ENDING THE THIRTIETH OF JUNE, EIGHTEEN HUNDRED AND FIFTY, AND FOR OTHER PURPOSES.

Repeal of proviso limiting the purchase of stocks by Treasury Department, 1847, ch. 5.

SEC. 3. *And be it further enacted,* That the proviso to the nineteenth section of the act of the twenty-eighth of January, eighteen hundred and forty-seven, entitled "An Act authorizing the issue of Treasury-notes, a loan, and for other purposes," be, and the same is hereby, repealed.

CHAP. I. — AN ACT TO AUTHORIZE THE ISSUE OF TREASURY-NOTES.

Dec. 23, 1857.

Vol. XI. p. 257.

Be it enacted by the Senate and House of Representatives of the United States of America in Congress assembled, That the President of the United States is hereby authorized to cause Treasury-notes for such sum or sums as the exigencies of the public service may require, but not to exceed, at any time, the amount of twenty millions of dollars, and of denominations not less than one hundred dollars for any such note, to be prepared, signed, and issued in the manner hereinafter provided.

Issue of not over $20,000,000 authorized in denominations of not less than $100 each. 1859, ch. 82, sec. 5.

SEC. 2. *And be it further enacted,* That such Treasury-notes shall be paid and redeemed by the United States at the Treasury thereof after the expiration of one year from the dates of said notes, from which dates, until they shall be respectively paid and redeemed, they shall bear such rate of interest as shall be expressed in said notes, which rate of interest upon the first issue, which shall not exceed six millions of dollars of such notes, shall be fixed by the Secretary of the Treasury, with the approbation of the President, but shall in no case exceed the rate of six per centum per annum. The residue shall be issued, in whole or in part, after public advertisement of not less than thirty days, as the Secretary of the Treasury may direct, by exchanging them at their par value for specie to the bidder or bidders who shall agree to make such exchange at the lowest rate of interest, not exceeding six per centum, upon the said notes: *Provided,* That, after the maturity of any of said notes, interest thereon shall cease at the expiration of sixty days' notice of readiness to pay and redeem the same, which may at any time or times be given by the Secretary of the Treasury, in one or more newspapers published at the seat of government. The payment or redemption of said notes herein provided shall be made to the lawful holders thereof, respectively, upon presentment at the Treasury, and shall include the principal of each note and the interest which shall be due thereon. And for such payment and redemption, at the time or times herein specified, the faith of the United States is hereby solemnly pledged.

How, when, where, and to whom issued, paid, and redeemed.

First issue not to exceed $6,000,000.

Rate of interest not over 6 per cent.

Residue how issued.

Proviso.

Interest when to cease.

Faith of the United States pledged for their redemption.

Form and signa-
tures.

SEC. 3. *And be it further enacted*, That such Treasury-notes shall be prepared under the direction of the Secretary of the Treasury, and shall be signed, in behalf of the United States, by the Treasurer thereof, and countersigned

Separate ac-
counts of each note
to be kept by the
Treasurer and by
the Register.

by the Register of the Treasury. Each of these officers shall keep, in a book or books provided for that purpose, separate, full, and accurate accounts, showing the number, date, amount, and rate of interest of each Treasury-note signed and countersigned by them, respectively; and also similar accounts showing all such notes as may be paid, redeemed, and cancelled, as the same may be returned;

Accounts of notes
paid and cancelled
to be preserved.

Treasurer to ac-
count quarterly.

all which accounts shall be carefully preserved in the Treasury Department. And the Treasurer shall account quarterly for all such Treasury-notes as shall have been countersigned by the Register, and delivered to the Treasurer for issue.

To be issued in
payment of public
creditors, or for
loans.

SEC. 4. *And be it further enacted*, That the Secretary of the Treasury is hereby authorized, with the approbation of the President, to cause such portion of said Treasury-notes as may be deemed expedient to be issued by the Treasurer in payment of warrants in favor of public creditors, or other persons lawfully entitled to such payment, who may choose to receive such notes in payment at par. And the Secretary of the Treasury is further authorized, with the approbation of the President, to borrow, from time to time, such sums of money upon the credit of such

Proviso.

Not to be dis-
posed of for less
than the principal
and interest.

notes as the President may deem expedient: *Provided*, That no Treasury-notes shall be pledged, hypothecated, sold, or disposed of in any way, for any purpose whatever, either directly or indirectly, for any sum less than the amount of such notes, including the principal and interest thereof.

Transferable by
indorsement and
delivery.

SEC. 5. *And be it further enacted*, That said Treasury-notes shall be transferable, by assignment indorsed thereon by the person to whose order the same shall be made payable, accompanied together with the delivery of the notes so assigned.

To be received
by public officers
for all dues to the
United States.

SEC. 6. *And be it further enacted*, That said Treasury-notes shall be received by the proper officers in payment of all duties and taxes laid by the authority of the United States, of all public lands sold by said authority, and of all debts to the United States of any character whatever, which may be due and payable at the time when said Treasury-notes may be offered in payment thereof; and upon every such payment, credit shall be given for the amount of principal and interest due on the note or notes received in payment, on the day when the same shall have been received by such officer.

SEC. 7. *And be it further enacted*, That every collector of the customs, receiver of public moneys, or other officer or agent of the United States, who shall receive any Treasury-note or notes in payment on account of the United States, shall take from the holder of such note or notes a receipt, upon the back of each, stating distinctly the date of such payment and the amount allowed upon such note; and every such officer or agent shall keep regular and specific entries of all Treasury-notes received in payment, showing the person from whom received, the number, date, and amount of principal and interest allowed on each and every Treasury-note received in payment; which entries shall be delivered to the Treasury, with the Treasury-note or notes mentioned therein, and, if found correct, such officer or agent shall receive credit for the amount, as provided in the last section of this act.

Receipt to be taken and entries made and allowed accordingly to officers.

SEC. 8. *And be it further enacted*, That the Secretary of the Treasury be, and he hereby is, authorized to make and issue, from time to time, such instructions, rules, and regulations to the several collectors, receivers, depositaries, and all others who may be required to receive such Treasury-notes in behalf of, and as agents in any capacity for, the United States, as to the custody, disposal, cancelling, and return of any such notes as may be paid to and received by them, respectively, and as to the accounts and returns to be made to the Treasury Department of such receipts as he shall deem best calculated to promote the public convenience and security, and to protect the United States, as well as individuals, from fraud and loss.

Secretary of Treasury to issue instructions, &c. to officers.

SEC. 9. *And be it further enacted*, That the Secretary of the Treasury be, and he hereby is, authorized and directed to cause to be paid the principal and interest of such Treasury-notes as may be issued under this act, at the time and times when, according to its provisions. the same

Payment and purchase.

should be paid. And the said Secretary is further author.
ized to purchase said notes at par for the amount of principal and interest due at the time of the purchase on such

Appropriation therefor. notes. And so much of any unappropriated money in the
Treasury as may be necessary for the purpose is hereby
appropriated to the payment of the principal and interest
of said notes.

May be issued in place of those re-deemed. ·SEC. 10. *And be it further enacted,* That, in place of
such Treasury-notes as may have been paid and redeemed,
other Treasury-notes to the same amount may be issued:

Total outstanding at no time to ex-ceed $20,000,000. *Provided,* That the aggregate sum outstanding, under the
authority of this act, shall at no time exceed twenty mil-
lions of dollars : *And provided, further,* That·the power to

Not to be issued after Jan. 1, 1859. *Post*, 1859, ch. 82, sec. 5. issue and reissue Treasury-notes, conferred on the President of the United States by this act, shall cease and de-
termine on the first day of January, eighteen hundred
and fifty-nine.

SEC. 11. *And be it further enacted,* That, to defray the
expenses of engraving, printing, preparing, and issuing the
Treasury-notes herein authorized, the sum of twenty thousand dollars is hereby appropriated, to be paid out of any

No compensation to any salaried offi-cer therefor. unappropriated money in the Treasury : *Provided,* That
no compensation shall be made to any officer whose salary
is fixed by law, for preparing, signing, or issuing Treasury-
notes.

!The forging, &c. thereof, or the pass-ing, &c., or the at-tempting to pass, &c., forged notes, made a felony. SEC. 12. *And be it further enacted,* That if any person
shall falsely make, forge, or counterfeit, or cause or pro-
cure to be falsely made, forged, or counterfeited, or willingly aid or assist in falsely making, forging, or counterfeiting, any note in imitation of, or purporting to be, a
Treasury-note, issued as aforesaid, or shall pass, utter, or
publish, or attempt to pass, utter, or publish, as true, any
false, forged, or counterfeited note, purporting to be a
Treasury-note as aforesaid, knowing the same to be falsely
made, forged, or counterfeited, or shall falsely alter, or
cause or procure to be falsely altered, or willingly aid or
assist in falsely altering, any Treasury-note issued as aforesaid, or shall pass, utter, or publish, or attempt to pass,
utter, or publish, as true, any falsely altered Treasury-
note, issued as aforesaid, knowing the same to be falsely
altered, every such person shall be deemed and adjudged

guilty of felony, and, being thereof convicted by due course of law, shall be sentenced to be imprisoned and kept at hard labor for a period not less than three years, nor more than ten years, and to be fined in a sum not exceeding five thousand dollars. *Penalty.*

SEC. 13. *And be it further enacted,* That if any person shall make or engrave, or cause or procure to be made or engraved, or shall have in his custody and possession, any metallic plate engraved after the similitude of any plate from which any notes issued as aforesaid shall have been printed, with intent to use such plate, or cause or suffer the same to be used, in forging or counterfeiting any of the notes issued as aforesaid, or shall have in custody or possession any blank note or notes engraved and printed after the similitude of any notes issued as aforesaid, with intent to use such blanks, or cause or suffer the same to be used in forging or counterfeiting any of the notes issued as aforesaid, or shall have in his custody or possession any paper adapted to the making of such notes, and similar to the paper upon which any such notes shall have been issued, with intent to use such paper, or cause or suffer the same to be used, in forging or counterfeiting any of the notes issued as aforesaid, every such person, being thereof convicted by due course of law, shall be sentenced to be imprisoned and kept to hard labor for a term not less than three nor more than ten years, and fined in a sum not exceeding five thousand dollars. *The engraving or possession, &c., of an engraved plate, or the possession of blank notes or paper for making such notes, with intent, &c., punishable by fine and imprisonment.*

SEC. 14. *And be it further enacted,* That it shall be the duty of the Secretary of the Treasury to cause a statement to be published monthly of the amount of Treasury-notes issued and paid and redeemed under the provisions of this act, showing the balance outstanding each month. *Monthly statement of notes issued, paid, and redeemed, to be published.*

Approved December 23, 1857.

June 14, 1858.
Vol. II. p. 365.
CHAP. CLXV.—AN ACT TO AUTHORIZE A LOAN NOT EX-
CEEDING THE SUM OF TWENTY MILLIONS OF DOLLARS.

1859, ch. 82, § 6.

*Be it enacted by the Senate and House of Representatives
of the United States of America in Congress assembled,*

President within twelve months may borrow not over $20,000,000, payable at any time after fifteen years from Jan. 1, 1859.
That the President of the United States be, and hereby is,
authorized, at any time within twelve months from the
passage of this act, to borrow, on the credit of the United
States, a sum not exceeding twenty millions of dollars, or
so much thereof as in his opinion the exigencies of the
public service may require, to be applied to the payment
of appropriations made by law, in addition to the money
received, or which may be received, into the Treasury

Proviso.
from other sources: *Provided,* That no stipulation or contract shall be made to prevent the United States from
reimbursing any sum borrowed under the authority of this
act at any time after the expiration of fifteen years from
the first day of January next.

Stock issued therefor shall bear not over five per cent interest, payable semi-annually, with coupons.
SEC. 2. *And be it further enacted,* That stock shall be
issued for the amount so borrowed, bearing interest not
exceeding five per centum per annum, payable semi-annually, with coupons for the semi-annual interest attached
to the certificates of stock thus created, and the Secretary
of the Treasury be, and hereby is, authorized, with the
Certificates, how prepared and signed, and amount of.
consent of the President, to cause certificates of stock to
be prepared, which shall be signed by the Register, and
sealed with the seal of the Treasury Department, for the
amount so borrowed, in favor of the parties lending the
Post, p. 430.
same, or their assigns: *Provided,* that no certificate shall
be issued for a less sum than one thousand dollars.

Loan to be advertized.
SEC. 3. *And be it further enacted,* That, before awarding said loan, the Secretary of the Treasury shall cause to
be inserted in two of the public newspapers of the city of
Washington, and in one or more public newspapers in
Notice
other cities of the United States, public notice that sealed
proposals for such loan will be received until a certain day
to be specified in such notice, not less than thirty days
from its first insertion in a Washington newspaper; and
such notice shall state the amount of the loan, at what
periods the money shall be paid, if by instalments, and at

what places. Such sealed proposals shall be opened on Proposals to be opened. the day appointed in the notice, in the presence of such persons as may choose to attend, and the proposals decided on by the Secretary of the Treasury, who shall accept the most favorable proposals offered by responsible bidders for said stock; and the said Secretary shall report to Congress, Secretary to report to Congress at commencement of its next session amount borrowed, &c. at the commencement of the next session, the amount of money borrowed under this act, and of whom, and on what terms, it shall have been obtained; with an abstract or brief statement of all the proposals submitted for the same, distinguishing between those accepted and those rejected, with a detailed statement of the expenses of making such loans: *Provided,* That no stock shall be dis- Stock not to be disposed of at less than par. posed of at less than its par value.

SEC. 4. *And be it further enacted,* That the faith of the Faith of the U. States pledged for its payment. United States is hereby pledged for the due payment of the interest and the redemption of the principal of said stock.

SEC. 5. *And be it further enacted,* That, to defray the Engraving, &c., certificates of stock. expenses of engraving and printing certificates of such stock, and other expenses incident to the execution of this act, the sum of five thousand dollars is hereby appropri- ated: *Provided,* That no compensation shall be allowed Proviso. for any service performed under this act to any officer whose salary is established by law.

Approved June 14, 1858.

CHAP. LXXXII. — AN ACT MAKING APPROPRIATIONS FOR *March* 3, 1859. SUNDRY CIVIL EXPENSES OF THE GOVERNMENT FOR THE Vol. XI. p. 430. YEAR ENDING THE THIRTIETH OF JUNE, EIGHTEEN HUN- DRED AND SIXTY.

SEC. 5. *And be it further enacted,* That the power to Authority to issue and reissue Treasury-notes under act 1857, ch. 1, extended to July 1, 1860. issue and reissue Treasury-notes, conferred on the Presi- dent of the United States by the act entitled "An act to authorize the issue of Treasury-notes," approved the twenty-third December, eighteen hundred and fifty-seven, be, and the same hereby is, revived and continued in force from the passage of this act until the first day of July,

Expenses thereof. eighteen hundred and sixty; and to defray the expenses
thereof the sum of five thousand dollars is hereby appro-
Proviso. priated: *Provided,* That the said notes may be issued
bearing an interest not exceeding six per centum per annum, and that it shall not be necessary, as directed by
the original act aforesaid, after advertisement to exchange
them for specie to the bidder or bidders who shall agree to
make such exchange at the lowest rate of interest upon
said notes, and that in all other respects the reissue of
said Treasury-notes shall be subject to the terms and conditions of the act aforesaid.

Coupon or reg-
istered stock may SEC. 6. *And be it further enacted,* That the Secretary
be issued. 1858, of the Treasury is hereby authorized, under the act of
ch. 166.
June fourteenth, eighteen hundred and fifty-eight, to issue
coupon or registered stock, as the purchaser may elect.

June 22, 1860. CHAP. CLXXX. — AN ACT AUTHORIZING A LOAN AND
Vol. XII. p. 79. PROVIDING FOR THE REDEMPTION OF TREASURY-NOTES.
(See Act of 8th February, 1861, Section 5.)

*Be it enacted by the Senate and House of Representa-
tives of the United States of America in Congress assem-
$ 21,000,000 may bled,* That the President of the United States be, and
be borrowed to
redeem Treasury- hereby is, authorized, at any time within twelve months
notes, &c.
from the passage of this act, to borrow, on the credit of
the United States, a sum not exceeding twenty-one millions of dollars or so much thereof as in his opinion the
exigencies of the public service may require, to be used in
the redemption of Treasury-notes now outstanding, and to
replace in the Treasury any amount of said notes which
shall have been paid and received for public dues, and for
other purposes.

Stock to be is- SEC. 2. *And be it further enacted,* That stock shall be
sued at interest of
not over six per issued for the amount so borrowed, bearing interest not
cent.
exceeding six per centum per annum, and to be reimbursed within a period not beyond twenty years, and not
Certificates. less than ten years; and the Secretary of the Treasury be,
and is hereby authorized, with the consent of the President, to cause certificates of stock to be prepared, which

shall be signed by the Register, and sealed with the seal of the Treasury Department, for the amount so borrowed, in favor of the parties lending the same, or their assigns, which certificates may be transferred on the books of the Treasury, under such regulations as may be established by the Secretary of the Treasury: *Provided,* That no certificate shall be issued for a less sum than one thousand dollars; *And provided, also,* That, whenever required, the Secretary of the Treasury may cause coupons of semi-annual interest payable thereon to be attached to certificates issued under this act; and any certificate with such coupons of interest attached may be assigned and transferred by delivery of the same, instead of being transferred on the books of the Treasury.

To be in sums of not less than $1000.

With coupons when required. Assignment thereof.

SEC. 3. *And be it further enacted,* That, before awarding said loan, the Secretary of the Treasury shall cause to be inserted in two of the public newspapers of the city of Washington, and in one or more public newspapers in other cities of the United States, public notice that sealed proposals for such loan will be received until a certain day, to be specified in such notice, not less than thirty days from its first insertion in a Washington newspaper; and such notice shall state the amount of the loan, at what periods the money shall be paid, if by instalments, and at what places. Such sealed proposals shall be opened on the day appointed in the notice, in the presence of such persons as may choose to attend, and the proposals decided by the Secretary of the Treasury, who shall accept the most favorable offered by responsible bidders for such stock, and the said Secretary shall report to Congress, at the commencement of the next session, the amount of money borrowed under this act, and of whom, and on what terms, it shall have been obtained, with an abstract or brief statement of all the proposals submitted for the same, distinguishing between those accepted and those rejected, with a detailed statement of the expense of making such loans: *And provided,* That no stock shall be disposed of at less than its par value; and the sum of five thousand dollars is hereby appropriated, out of any money in the Treasury not otherwise appropriated, to pay for engraving and printing the certificates, and other expenses of exe-

Proposals to be advertised for.

When to be opened, and what bids accepted.

Report to Congress.

Stock not to be disposed of at less than par.

Appropriation for expenses under this act.

c *

cuting this act; but no additional compensation shall be
allowed to any person receiving a salary by law.

Faith of the U.
States pledged.

SEC. 4. *And be it further enacted,* That the faith of the
United States is hereby pledged for the due payment of
the interest and the redemption of the principal of said
stock.

Approved June 22, 1860.

Dec. 17, 1860.
Vol. XII. p. 121.

CHAP. I. — AN ACT TO AUTHORIZE THE ISSUE OF TREASURY-
NOTES, AND FOR OTHER PURPOSES. (See Act of 8th
February, 1861, Section 5.)

*Be it enacted by the Senate and House of Representatives
of the United States of America in Congress assembled,*

Treasury-notes,
how to be issued,
amount, and de-
nomination.

That the President of [the] United [States] be herely
authorized to cause Treasury-notes, for such sum or sums
as the exigencies of the public service may require, but
not to exceed at any time the amount of ten millions of
dollars, and of denominations not less than fifty dollars for
any such note, to be prepared, signed, and issued in the
manner hereinafter provided.

To be redeemed
one year from their
date.

SEC. 2. *And be it further enacted,* That such Treasury-
notes shall be paid and redeemed by the United States, at
the Treasury thereof, after the expiration of one year from
the date of issue of such notes; from which dates, until
they shall be respectively paid and redeemed, they shall
bear such rate of interest as shall be expressed in such

Rate of interest,
and when interest
to cease.

notes, which rate of interest shall be six per centum per
annum: *Provided,* That, after the maturity of any of said
notes, interest thereon shall cease at the expiration of
sixty days' notice of readiness to redeem and pay the same,
which may at any time or times be given by the Secretary
of the Treasury, in one or more newspapers at the seat of
government. The redemption and payment of said notes,

Who to receive
payment.

herein provided, shall be made to the lawful holders thereof
respectively upon presentment at the Treasury, and shall
include the principal of each note and the interest which
shall be due thereon. And for the payment and redemp-

tion of such notes at the time and times therein specified, the faith of the United States is hereby solemnly pledged.

Faith of the U. States pledged.

SEC. 3. *And be it further enacted,* That such Treasury-notes shall be prepared under the direction of the Secretary of the Treasury, and shall be signed in behalf of the United States by the Treasurer thereof, and countersigned by the Register of the Treasury. Each of these officers shall keep, in a book or books provided for the purpose, separate, full, and accurate accounts, showing the number, date, amount, and rate of interest of each Treasury-note signed and countersigned by them respectively ; and, also, similar accounts showing all such notes which may be paid, redeemed, and cancelled, as the same may be returned ; all which accounts shall be carefully preserved in the Treasury Department. And the Treasurer shall account quarterly for all such Treasury-notes as shall have been countersigned by the Register and delivered to the Treasurer for issue.

Notes, how signed.

Account of notes to be kept.

Treasurer to account quarterly.

SEC. 4. *And be it further enacted,* That the Secretary of the Treasury is hereby authorized, with the approbation of the President, to cause such portion of said Treasury-notes as may be deemed expedient to be issued by the Treasurer in payment of warrants in favor of public creditors, or other persons lawfully entitled to payment, who may choose to receive such notes in payment. at par ; and the Secretary of the Treasury is hereby authorized, with the approbation of the President, to issue the notes hereby authorized to be issued, at such rate of interest as may be offered by the lowest responsible bidder or bidders, who may agree to take the said notes at par after public advertisement of not less than ten days in such papers as the President may direct, the said advertisement to propose to issue such notes at par to those who may offer to take the same at the lowest rate of interest. But in deciding upon those bids, no fraction shall be considered which may be less than one fourth per centum per annum.

Notes may be issued at par to pay public creditors.

Rate of interest on such notes, how to be determined.

SEC. 5. *And be it further enacted,* That said Treasury-notes shall be transferable by assignment indorsed thereon by the person to whose order the same may be made payable, accompanied together with the delivery of the note so assigned.

Transferable by indorsement and delivery.

SEC. 6. *And be it further enacted,* That said Treasury-notes shall be received by the proper officers in payment of all duties and taxes laid by the authority of the United States, of all public lands sold by said authority, and of all debts to the United States, of any character whatever, which may be due and payable at the time when said Treasury-notes may be offered in payment thereof; and

upon every such payment credit shall be given for the amount of principal and interest due on the note or notes received in payment, on the day when the same shall have been received by such officer.

SEC. 7. *And be it further enacted,* That every collector of customs, receiver of public moneys, or other officer or agent of the United States, who shall receive any Treasury-note or notes in payment on account of the United States, shall take from the holder of such note or notes a receipt on the back of each, stating distinctly the date of such payment, and the amount allowed on such note ; and every such officer or agent shall keep regular and specific entries of all Treasury-notes received in payment, showing the person from whom received, the number, date, and amount of principal and interest allowed on each and every Treasury-note received in payment, which entries shall be delivered to the Treasury with the Treasury-note or notes mentioned therein ; and, if found correct, such officer or agent shall receive credit for the amount, as provided in the sixth section of this act.

SEC. 8. *And be it further enacted,* That the Secretary of the Treasury be, and hereby is, authorized to make and issue from time to time such instructions, rules, and regulations to the several collectors, receivers, depositaries, and all others who may be required to receive such Treasury-notes in behalf of, and as agents in any capacity for, the United States, as to the custody, disposal, cancelling, and return of any such notes as may be paid to, and received by, them respectively, and as to the accounts and returns to be made to the Treasury Department of such receipts, as he shall deem best calculated to promote the public convenience and security, and to protect the United States, as well as individuals, from fraud and loss.

SEC. 9. *And be it further enacted,* That the Secretary

of the Treasury be, and hereby is, authorized and directed to cause to be paid, the principal and interest of such Treasury-notes as may be issued under this act, at the time and times when, according to its provisions, the same should be paid. And said Secretary is further authorized to purchase said notes at par for the amount of principal and interest due thereon at the time of such purchase. And so much of any unappropiated money in the Treasury as may be necessary for the purpose is hereby appropriated for the payment of the principal and interest of said notes.

SEC. 10. *And be it further enacted,* That, in place of such Treasury-notes as may have been paid and redeemed, other Treasury-notes to the same amount may be issued : *Provided,* That the aggregate sum outstanding under the authority of this act shall at no time exceed the sum of ten millions of dollars : *And provided further,* That the power to issue and reissue Treasury-notes conferred by this act shall cease and determine on the first day of January, in the year eighteen hundred and sixty-three.

SEC. 11. *And be it further enacted,* That, to defray the expense of engraving, printing, preparing, and issuing the Treasury-notes herein authorized, the sum of fifteen thousand dollars is hereby appropriated, payable out of any unappropiated money in the Treasury : *Provided,* That no compensation shall be made to any officer whose salary is fixed by law, for preparing, signing, or issuing Treasury-notes.

SEC. 12. *And be it further enacted,* That if any person shall falsely make, forge, or counterfeit, or cause or procure to be made, forged, or counterfeited, or willingly aid or assist in falsely making, forging, or counterfeiting, any note in imitation of, or purporting to be, a Treasury-note issued as aforesaid, or shall pass, utter, or publish, or attempt to pass, utter, or publish, any false, forged, or counterfeited note, purporting to be a Treasury-note as aforesaid, knowing the same to be falsely made, forged, or counterfeited, or shall falsely alter, or cause or procure to be falsely altered, or willingly aid or assist in falsely altering any Treasury-note issued as aforesaid, or shall pass, utter, or publish, or attempt to pass, utter, or publish

5

as true, any falsely altered Treasury-note, issued as aforesaid, knowing the same to be falsely altered, every such person shall be deemed and adjudged guilty of felony, and, being thereof convicted by due course of law, shall be sentenced to be imprisoned and kept at hard labor for a period not less than three years nor more than ten years, and to be fined in a sum not exceeding five thousand dollars.

Engraving plate to print forged notes, how punished.

SEC. 13. *And be it further enacted,* That if any person shall make or engrave, or cause to procure to be made or engraved, or shall have in his custody and possession, any metallic plate engraved after the similitude of any plate from which any notes issued as aforesaid shall have been printed, with intent to use such plate, or cause or suffer the same to be used, in forging or counterfeiting any of

Possession of blank notes, with intent, &c.

the notes issued as aforesaid, or shall have in his custody or possession any blank note or notes engraved and printed after the similitude of any notes issued as aforesaid, with intent to use such blanks, or cause or suffer the same to be used, in forging or counterfeiting any of the notes issued as aforesaid, or shall have in his custody or possession any paper adapted to the making of such notes, and similar to the paper upon which any such notes shall have been issued, with intent to use such paper, or cause or suffer the same to be used, in forging or counterfeiting any of the notes issued as aforesaid, every such person, being thereof convicted by due course of law, shall be sentenced to be imprisoned and kept to hard labor for a term not less than three nor more than ten years, and fined in a sum not exceeding five thousand dollars.

Secretary of the Treasury to publish a statement monthly.

SEC. 14. *And be it further enacted,* That it shall be the duty of the Secretary of the Treasury to cause a statement to be published monthly of the amount of Treasury-notes issued and paid and redeemed under the provisions of this act, showing the balance outstanding each month.

Money hereafter contracted for under act of 1860, ch. 180, to be applied to redemption of Treasury-notes.

SEC. 15. *And be it further enacted,* That all moneys hereafter contracted for under the authority of the act entitled "An act authorizing a loan, and providing for the redemption of Treasury-notes," approved June twenty-second, eighteen hundred and sixty, shall be used in the redemption of Treasury-notes now outstanding, and those to be issued under this act, and to replace in the Treasury any amount of said notes which shall have been paid and received for public dues, and for no other purpose.

Approved December 17, 1860.

CHAP. XXIX. — AN ACT AUTHORIZING A LOAN.

February 8, 1861.
Vol. XII. p. 129.

Be it enacted by the Senate and House of Representatives of the United States of America in Congress assembled, That the President of the United States be, and hereby is, authorized, at any time before the first of July next, to borrow, on the credit of the United States, a sum not exceeding twenty-five millions of dollars, or so much thereof as in his opinion the exigencies of the public service may require to be used in the payment of the current demands upon the Treasury, and for the redemption of Treasury-notes now outstanding, and to replace in the Treasury any amount of said notes which shall have been paid and received for public dues.

$25,000,000 loan authorized before July 1, 1861.

Purpose of loan.

SEC. 2. *And be it further enacted,* That stock shall be issued for the amount so borrowed, bearing interest not exceeding six per centum per annum, and to be reimbursed within a period not beyond twenty years, and not less than ten years ; and the Secretary of the Treasury be, and is, hereby authorized, with the consent of the President, to cause certificates of stock to be prepared, which shall be signed by the Register and sealed with the seal of the Treasury Department, for the amount so borrowed, in favor of the parties lending the same, or their assigns, which certificates may be transferred on the books of the Treasury, under such regulations as may be established by the Secretary of the Treasury : *Provided,* That no certificate shall be issued for a less sum than one thousand dollars : *And provided, also,* That, whenever required, the Secretary of the Treasury may cause coupons of semi-annual interest payable thereon to be attached to certificates issued under this act ; and any certificate with such coupons of interest attached may be assigned and transferred by delivery of the same, instead of being transferred on the books of the Treasury.

Stock, issue, form, interest, transfer, &c., of.

No certificate to be for less than $1,000.

Interest coupons may be attached.

Proposals for loans to be advertised for. SEC. 3. *And be it further enacted,* That, before awarding said loan, the Secretary of the Treasury shall cause to be inserted in two of the public newspapers of the city of Washington, and in one or more public newspapers in other cities of the United States, public notice that sealed proposals for such a loan will be received until a certain day, to be specified in such notice, not less than ten days from its first insertion in a Washington newspaper ; and such notice shall state the amount of the loan, at what periods the money shall be paid, if by instalments, and at **When, where, and how to be opened.** what places. Such sealed proposals shall be opened, on the day appointed in the notice, in the presence of such persons as may choose to attend, and the proposals decided by the Secretary of the Treasury, who shall accept the most favorable offered by responsible bidders for said stock. And the said Secretary shall report to Congress, at the commencement of the next session, the amount of money borrowed under this act, and of whom, and on what terms, it shall have been obtained, with an abstract or brief statement of all the proposals submitted for the same, distinguishing between those accepted and those rejected, with a detailed statement of the expense of making such loans.

Faith of the U. States pledged. SEC. 4. *And be it further enacted,* That the faith of the United States is hereby pledged for the due payment of ————, the interest and the redemption of the principal of said stock.

Residue of loan under act of 1860, ch. 180, how to be applied SEC. 5. *And be it further enacted,* That the residue of the loan authorized by the act of twenty-second of June, eighteen hundred and sixty, or so much thereof as is necessary, shall be applied to the redemption of the Treasury-notes issued under the act of seventeenth of December, eighteen hundred and sixty, and for no other purpose ; **Bonds under act of 1860, ch. 180, may be exchanged at par for Treasury-notes.** and the Secretary of the Treasury is hereby authorized, at his discretion, to exchange at par bonds of the United States, authorized by said act of twenty-second June, eighteen hundred and sixty, for the said Treasury-notes, and the accruing interest thereon.

Appropriation for expenses under this act. SEC. 6. *And be it further enacted,* That to defray the expense of engraving and printing certificates of such stock, and other expenses incident to the execution of this act, the sum of twenty thousand dollars is hereby appropriated : *Provided,* That no compensation shall be allowed for any service performed under this act to any officer whose salary is established by law.

SEC. 7. *And be it further enacted,* That the Secretary of the Treasury shall not be obliged to accept the most favorable bids as hereinbefore provided, unless he shall consider it advantageous to the United States to do so, but for any portion of such loan, not taken under the first advertisement, he may advertise again at his discretion. Secretary of the Treasury need not accept bids unless, &c.

Approved February 8, 1861.

CHAP. LXVIII. — AN ACT TO PROVIDE FOR THE PAYMENT OF OUTSTANDING TREASURY-NOTES, TO AUTHORIZE A LOAN, TO REGULATE AND FIX THE DUTIES ON IMPORTS, AND FOR OTHER PURPOSES. *March 2, 1861.* Vol. XII. p. 178.

Be it enacted by the Senate and House of Representatives of the United States of America in Congress assembled, That the President of the United States be, and hereby is, authorized at any time within twelve months from the passage of this act to borrow, on the credit of the United States, a sum not exceeding ten millions of dollars, or so much thereof as in his opinion the exigencies of the public service may require, to be applied to the payment of appropriations made by law, and the balance of Treasury-notes now outstanding, and no other purposes, in addition to the money received, or which may be received, into the Treasury from other sources : *Provided,* That no stipulation or contract shall be made to prevent the United States from reimbursing any sum borrowed under the authority of this act at any time after the expiration of ten years from the first day of July next, by the United States giving three months notice, to be published in some newspaper published at the seat of government, of their readiness to do so ; and no contract shall be made to prevent the redemption of the same at any time after the expiration of twenty years from the said first day of July next, without notice. President may borrow within 12 months, not over $10,000,000. How to be applied. When to be redeemed.

D

Stock, issue, certificates, rate of interest, transferable.

SEC. 2. *And be it further enacted,* That stock shall be issued for the amount so borrowed, bearing interest not exceeding six per centum per annum; and the Secretary of the Treasury be, and is hereby authorized, with the consent of the President, to cause certificates of stock to be prepared, which shall be signed by the Register and sealed with the seal of the Treasury Department, for the amount so borrowed, in favor of the parties lending the same, or their assigns, which certificates may be transferred on the books of the Treasury, under such regulations as may be established by the Secretary of the

Certificates to be for not less than $1,000.

Treasury: *Provided,* That no certificate shall be issued for a less sum than one thousand dollars: *And provided,*

Coupons may be attached.

also, That, whenever required, the Secretary of the Treasury may cause coupons of semi-annual interest, payable thereon, to be attached to certificates issued under this act; and any certificate with such coupons of interest attached may be assigned and transferred by delivery of the same, instead of being transferred on the books of the Treasury.

Proposals for loan to be advertised for.

SEC. 3. *And be it further enacted,* That, before awarding any of said loan, the Secretary of the Treasury shall, as the exigencies of the public service require, cause to be inserted in two of the public newspapers of the city of Washington, and in one or more public newspapers in other cities of the United States, public notice that sealed proposals for so much of said loan as is required will be received until a certain day, to be specified in such notice,

Notice.

not less than thirty days from its first insertion in a Washington newspaper; and such notice shall state the amount of the loan, at what periods the money shall be paid, if by

When to be opened.

instalments, and at what place. Such sealed proposals shall be opened on the day appointed in the notice, in the presence of such persons as may choose to attend, and the

Which to be accepted.

proposals decided on by the Secretary of the Treasury, who shall accept the most favorable offered by responsible

Report to be made to Congress.

bidders for said stock. And the said Secretary shall report to Congress, at the commencement of the next session, the amount of money borrowed under this act, and of whom, and on what terms, it shall have been obtained, with an abstract or brief statement of all the proposals submitted for the same, distinguishing between those accepted and those rejected, with a detailed statement of the expenses of making such loans: *Provided,* That no stock shall be disposed of at less than its par value: *And provided, further,* That no part of the loan hereby authorized shall be applied to the service of the present fiscal year.

No stock to be sold for less than par.

Loan, how applied.

SEC. 4. *And be it further enacted,* That in case the proposals made for said loan, or for so much thereof as the exigencies of the public service shall require, shall not be satisfactory, the President of the United States shall be, and hereby is, authorized to decline to accept such offer if for less than the par value of the bonds constituting the said stock, and in lieu thereof, and to the extent and amount of the loan authorized to be made by this act, to issue Treasury-notes for sums not less than fifty dollars, bearing interest at the rate of six per centum per annum, payable semi-annually on the first days of January and July in each year, at proper places of payment to be prescribed by the Secretary, with the approval of the President; and under the like circumstances and conditions, the President of the United States is hereby authorized to substitute Treasury-notes of equal amount for the whole or any part of any of the loans for which he is now by law authorized to contract and issue bonds. And the Treasury-notes so issued under the authority herein given, shall be received in payment for all debts due to the United States when offered, and in like manner shall be given in payment for any sum due from the United States, when payment in that mode is requested by the person to whom payment is to be made, or for their par value in coin. And the faith of the United States is hereby pledged for the due payment of the interest and the redemption of the principal of the stock or Treasury-notes which may be issued under the authority of this act; and the sum of twenty thousand dollars is hereby appropriated, out of any money in the Treasury not otherwise appropriated, to pay the expenses of preparing the certificates of stock or Treasury-notes herein authorized, to be done in the usual mode and under the restrictions as to employment and payment of offices contained in the laws authorizing for-

If proposals for loan are not satisfactory, Treasury-notes may be issued.

Amount when payable.

Faith of the U. States pledged

Appropriation for expenses.

May be exchanged for bonds, &c. mer loans and issues of Treasury-notes; and it shall be at the option of holders of the Treasury-notes hereby authorized by this act, to exchange the same for the stock herein authorized, at par, or for bonds, in lieu of which said

Proviso. Treasury-notes were issued : *Provided,* That no certificate shall be exchanged for Treasury-notes, or bonds, in sums less than five hundred dollars : *And provided, further,*

Notes not to be issued after June, 1862. That the authority to issue the said Treasury-notes, or give the same in payment for debts due from the United States, shall be limited to the thirtieth day of June, eighteen hundred and sixty-two; and that the same may be

Redemption. redeemable at the pleasure of the United States at any time within two years after the passage of this act; and

Interest. that said notes shall cease to bear interest after they shall have been called in by the Secretary of the Treasury under the provisions of this act.

July 17, 1861.
Vol. XII. p. 259.
CHAP. V. — AN ACT TO AUTHORIZE A NATIONAL LOAN, AND FOR OTHER PURPOSES.

Be it enacted by the Senate and House of Representatives of the United States of America in Congress assembled,

Secretary of the Treasury may borrow within twelve months not over $ 250,000,000. That the Secretary of the Treasury be, and he is hereby, authorized to borrow on the credit of the United States, within twelve months from the passage of this act, a sum not exceeding two hundred and fifty millions of dollars, or so much thereof as he may deem necessary for the public

Coupon or registered bonds or Treasury - notes may be issued therefor. service, for which he is authorized to issue coupon bonds, or registered bonds, or Treasury-notes, in such proportions of each as he may deem advisable; the bonds to bear interest not exceeding seven per centum per annum, payable

Bonds when redeemable. semi-annually, irredeemable for twenty years, and after that period redeemable at the pleasure of the United States; and

Treasury - notes; denomination ; interest; when payable. the Treasury-notes to be of any denomination fixed by the Secretary of the Treasury, not less than fifty dollars, and to be payable three years after date, with interest at the rate of seven and three tenths per centum per annum,

Certain Treasury-notes may be issued in exchange for coin, &c. payable semi-annually. And the Secretary of the Treasury may also issue in exchange for coin, and as part of the above loan, or may pay for salaries or other dues from the United States, Treasury-notes of a less denomination than fifty dollars, not bearing interest, but payable on demand by the Assistant Treasurers of the United States at Philadelphia, New York, or Boston, or Treasury-notes bearing interest at the rate of three and sixty-five hundredths per centum, payable in one year from date, and exchangeable at any time for Treasury-notes for fifty dollars and upwards, issuable under the authority of this act, and bearing interest as specified above : *Provided*, That no exchange of such notes in any less amount than one hundred dollars shall be made at any one time : *And provided further*, That no Treasury-notes shall be issued of a less denomination than ten dollars, and that the whole amount of Treasury-notes, not bearing interest, issued under the authority of this act, shall not exceed fifty millions of dollars. Proviso
Proviso.

SEC. 2. *And be it further enacted*, That the Treasury-notes and bonds issued under the provisions of this act shall be signed by the first or second Comptroller, or the Register of the Treasury, and countersigned by such other officer or officers of the Treasury as the Secretary of the Treasury may designate ; and all such obligations, of the denomination of fifty dollars and upwards, shall be issued under the seal of the Treasury Department. The registered bonds shall be transferable on the books of the Treasury on the delivery of the certificate, and the coupon bonds and Treasury-notes shall be transferable by delivery. The interest coupons may be signed by such person or persons, or executed in such manner, as may be designated by the Secretary of the Treasury, who shall fix the compensation for the same. Notes and bonds, how signed, &c.
How transferable.

SEC. 3. *And be it further enacted*, That the Secretary of the Treasury shall cause books to be opened for subscription to the Treasury-notes for fifty dollars and upwards at such places as he may designate in the United States, and under such rules and regulations as he may prescribe, to be superintended by the Assistant Treasurers of the United States at their respective localities, and at other places, by such depositaries, postmasters, and other persons as he may designate, notice thereof being given in Books to be opened for subscription for Treasury-notes for $50 and over, &c.

at least two daily papers of this city, and in one or more public newspapers published in the several places where

Who may subscribe. subscription-books may be opened; and subscriptions for such notes may be received from all persons who may desire to subscribe, any law to the contrary notwithstanding; and

If larger amount is subscribed, &c. if a larger amount shall be subscribed in the aggregate than is required at one time, the Secretary of the Treasury is authorized to receive the same, should he deem it advantageous to the public interest; and if not, he shall accept the amount required by giving the preference to the

Pay of those receiving subscriptions. smaller subscriptions; and the Secretary of the Treasury shall fix the compensations of the public officers or others designated for receiving said subscriptions: *Provided,*

Proviso. That for performing this or any other duty in connection with this act, no compensation for services rendered shall be allowed or paid to any public officer whose salary is

Payment of subscription. established by law; and the Secretary of the Treasury may also make such other rules and regulations as he may deem expedient touching the instalment to be paid on any subscription at the time of subscribing, and further payments by instalments or otherwise, and penalties for nonpayment of any instalment, and also concerning the receipt, deposit, and safe keeping of money received from such subscriptions, until the same can be placed in the possession of the official depositaries of the Treasury, any law or laws to the contrary notwithstanding. And the

Treasury-notes of $50 and upwards may be exchanged for coin, &c. Secretary of the Treasury is also authorized, if he shall deem it expedient, before opening books of subscription as above provided, to exchange for coin or pay for public dues or for Treasury-notes of the issue of twenty-third of December, eighteen hundred and fifty-seven, and falling due on the thirtieth of June, eighteen hundred and sixty-one, or for Treasury-notes issued and taken in exchange for such notes, any amount of said Treasury-notes for fifty dollars or upwards not exceeding one hundred millions of dollars.

Proposals for loan to be published. Sec. 4. *And be it further enacted,* That, before awarding any portion of the loan in bonds authorized by this act, the Secretary of the Treasury, if he deem it advisable to issue proposals for the same in the United States, shall give not less than fifteen days' public notice in two or more

of the public newspapers in the city of Washington, and
in such other places of the United States as he may deem
advisable, designating the amount of such loan, the place
and the time up to which sealed proposals will be received
for the same, the periods for the payment, and the amount
of each instalment in which it is to be paid, and the penalty for the non-payment of any such instalments, and
when and where such proposals shall be opened in the
presence of such persons as may choose to attend; and
the Secretary of the Treasury is authorized to accept the
most favorable proposals offered by responsible bidders : *Most favorable offers to be accept-*
Provided, That no offer shall be accepted at less than *ed, but at not less than par.*
par.

SEC. 5. *And be it further enacted,* That the Secretary *Portion of loan may be negotiated in foreign country.*
of the Treasury may, if he deem it advisable, negotiate
any portion of said loan, not exceeding one hundred millions of dollars, in any foreign country, and payable at any
designated place either in the United States or in Europe, *Proceedings in such case.*
and may issue registered or coupon bonds for the amount
thus negotiated, agreeably to the provisions of this act,
bearing interest payable semi-annually, either in the
United States or at any designated place in Europe; and
he is further authorized to appoint such agent or agents
as he may deem necessary for negotiating such loan under
his instructions, and for paying the interest on the same,
and to fix the compensation of such agent or agents, and
shall prescribe to them all the rules, regulations, and
modes under which such loans shall be negotiated, and
shall have power to fix the rate of exchange at which the
principal shall be received from the contractors for the
loan, and the exchange for the payment of the principal
and interest in Europe shall be at the same rate.

SEC. 6. *And be it further enacted,* That whenever any *Treasury-notes under $50 may be reissued prior to Dec. 31, 1862.*
Treasury-notes of a denomination less than fifty dollars,
authorized to be issued by this act, shall have been redeemed, the Secretary of the Treasury may reissue the
same, or may cancel them and issue new notes to an equal
amount: *Provided,* That the aggregate amounts of bonds *Proviso.*
and Treasury-notes issued under the foregoing provisions
of this act shall never exceed the full amount authorized
by the first section of this act; and the power to issue or

reissue such notes shall cease and determine after the thirty-first of December, eighteen hundred and sixty-two.

Treasury - notes may be issued in exchange for coin, &c.

SEC. 7. *And be it further enacted,* That the Secretary of the Treasury is hereby authorized, whenever he shall deem it expedient, to issue in exchange for coin, or in payment for public dues, Treasury-notes of any of the denominations hereinbefore specified, bearing interest not exceeding six per centum per annum, and payable at any time not exceeding twelve months from date, provided that the amount of notes so issued, or paid, shall at no time exceed twenty millions of dollars.

Secretary of the Treasury to report to Congress.

SEC. 8. *And be it further enacted,* That the Secretary of the Treasury shall report to Congress, immediately after the commencement of the next session, the amount he has borrowed under the provisions of this act, of whom, and on what terms, with an abstract of all the proposals, designating those that have been accepted and those that have been rejected, and the amount of bonds or Treasury-notes that have been issued for the same.

Faith of the U. States pledged.

SEC. 9. *And be it further enacted,* That the faith of the United States is hereby solemnly pledged for the payment of the interest, and redemption of the principal, of the loan authorized by this act.

Certain provisions of act of 1857, ch. 1, revived.

SEC. 10. *And be it further enacted,* That all the provisions of the act entitled "An Act to authorize the issue of Treasury-notes," approved the twenty-third day of December, eighteen hundred and fifty-seven, so far as the same can or may be applied to the provisions of this act, and not inconsistent therewith, are hereby revived or re-enacted.

Appropriation for expenses under this act.

SEC. 11. *And be it further enacted,* That, to defray all the expenses that may attend the execution of this act, the sum of two hundred thousand dollars, or so much thereof as may be necessary, be, and the same is hereby, appropriated, to be paid out of any money in the Treasury not otherwise appropriated.

Approved July 17, 1861.

CHAP. XLVI.—AN ACT SUPPLEMENTARY TO AN ACT EN- *August 5, 1861*
TITLED "AN ACT TO AUTHORIZE A NATIONAL LOAN, AND *Vol. XII. p. 313.*
FOR OTHER PURPOSES." *1861, ch. 5.*

Be it enacted by the Senate and House of Representa- Six per cent
tives of the United States of America in Congress assembled, bonds may be is-
That the Secretary of the Treasury is hereby authorized to exchangeable for
issue bonds of the United States, bearing interest at six notes.
per centum per annum, and payable at the pleasure of the
United States after twenty years from date; and if any
holder of Treasury-notes, bearing interest at the rate of
seven and three tenths per centum, which may be issued
under the authority of the act to authorize a national loan,
and for other purposes, approved July seventeenth, eighteen hundred and sixty-one, shall desire to exchange the
same for said bonds, the Secretary of the Treasury may,
at any time before or at the maturity of said Treasury- Denomination
notes, issue to said holder, in payment thereof, an amount bonds.
of said bonds equal to the amount which, at the time of
such payment or exchange, may be due on said Treasury-
notes; but no such bonds shall be issued for a sum less
than five hundred dollars, nor shall the whole amount of
such bonds exceed the whole amount of Treasury-notes
bearing seven and three tenths per centum interest, issued
under said act; and any part of the Treasury-notes pay- Where Treasury-
able on demand, authorized by said act, may be made pay- payable.
able by the Assistant Treasurer at St. Louis, or by the
depositary at Cincinnati.

SEC. 2. *And be it further enacted,* That the Treasury- Treasury-notes,
notes issued under the provisions of said act to authorize a
national loan, and for other purposes, or of any other act
now in force authorizing the issue of such notes, shall be
signed by the Treasurer of the United States, or by some
officer of the Treasury Department, designated by the
Secretary of the Treasury, for said Treasurer, and countersigned by the Register of the Treasury, or by some
officer of the Treasury Department, designated by the
Secretary of the Treasury, for said Register, and no Treas- Need not have
ury-notes, issued under any act, shall require the seal of seal.
the Treasury Department.

SEC. 3. *And be it further enacted,* That so much of the act to which this is supplementary as limits the denomination of a portion of the Treasury-notes authorized by said act at not less than ten dollars, be, and is, so modified as to authorize the Secretary of the Treasury to fix the denomination of said notes at not less than five dollars.

Appropriations for purposes of this act, &c. SEC. 4. *And be it further enacted,* That, in addition to the amount heretofore appropriated, the sum of one hundred thousand dollars, or so much thereof as may be necessary, be, and the same is hereby, appropriated, out of any money in the Treasury not otherwise appropriated, to pay such expenses, commissions, or compensation, as may be necessary, in the judgment of the Secretary of the Treasury, to carry into execution the provisions of this act, and of the act to which this is supplementary.

Notes on demand, &c., under $ 50, receivable for public dues. SEC. 5. *And be it further enacted,* That the Treasury-notes authorized by the act to which this is supplementary, of a less denomination than fifty dollars, payable on demand without interest, and not exceeding in amount the sum of fifty millions of dollars, shall be receivable in payment of public dues.

Portions of Sub-treasury Act suspended. SEC. 6. *And be it further enacted,* That the provisions of the act entitled "An Act to provide for the better organization of the Treasury, and for the collection, safe-keeping, and transfer, and disbursements of the public revenue," passed August six, eighteen hundred and forty-**1846, ch. 90.** six, be, and the same are hereby, suspended, so far as to allow the Secretary of the Treasury to deposit any of the moneys obtained on any of the loans now authorized by law, to the credit of the Treasurer of the United States, in such solvent specie-paying banks as he may select; and **Deposits in solvent specie-paying banks.** the said moneys, so deposited, may be withdrawn from such deposit for deposit with the regular authorized depositaries, or for the payment of public dues, or paid in redemption of the notes authorized to be issued under this act, or the act to which this is supplementary, payable on demand, as may seem expedient to, or be directed by, the Secretary of the Treasury.

Six per cent bonds due in 20 years may be issued for certain seven per cent bonds. SEC. 7. *And be it further enacted,* That the Secretary of the Treasury may sell or negotiate, for any portion of the loan provided for in the act to which this is supplementary, bonds payable not more than twenty years from date, and bearing interest not exceeding six per centum per annum, payable semi-annually, at any rate not less than the equivalent of par, for the bonds bearing seven per centum at interest, authorized by said act.

Approved August 5, 1861.

AN ACT TO AUTHORIZE AN ADDITIONAL ISSUE OF UNITED STATES NOTES. *Feb. 12, 1862.*

Be it enacted by the Senate and House of Representatives of the United States of America in Congress assembled, That the Secretary of the Treasury, in addition to the fifty millions of notes payable on demand of denominations not less than five dollars, heretofore authorized by the acts of July seventeenth and August fifth, eighteen hundred and sixty-one, be, and is hereby authorized to issue like notes, and for like purposes, to the amount of ten millions of dollars, and said notes shall be deemed part of the loan of two hundred and fifty millions of dollars, authorized by said act.

Authorizes the issue of $10,000,000 demand-notes additional.

To be part of loan of $ 250,000,000.

Approved February 12, 1862.

AN ACT TO AUTHORIZE THE ISSUE OF UNITED STATES NOTES, AND FOR THE REDEMPTION · OR FUNDING THEREOF, AND FOR FUNDING THE FLOATING DEBT OF THE UNITED STATES. *Feb. 25, 1862.*

Be it enacted by the Senate and House of Representatives of the United States of America in Congress assembled, That the Secretary of the Treasury is hereby authorized to issue, on the credit of the United States, one hundred and fifty millions of dollars of United States notes, not bearing interest, payable to bearer, at the Treasury of the United States, and of such denominations as he may deem expedient, not less than five dollars each : *Provided, however,* That fifty millions of said notes shall be in lieu of the demand Treasury-notes, authorized to be

$ 150,000,000 Treasury-notes authorized.

Not less than $ 5 each.

$50,000,000 to be in lieu of demand-notes, which are to be redeemed.

issued by the act of July seventeen, eighteen hundred and sixty-one ; which said demand-notes shall be taken up as rapidly as practicable, and the notes herein provided for substituted for them : *And provided further,* That the amount of the two kinds of notes together shall at no time exceed the sum of one hundred and fifty millions of dollars, and such notes herein authorized shall be receivable in payment of all taxes, internal duties, excises, debts, and

Receivable in payment of all dues to United States except duties on imports, and of claims against the United States except interest, and a legal tender in all cases of debt. demands of every kind due to the United States, except duties on imports, and of all claims and demands against the United States of every kind whatsoever, except for interest upon bonds and notes, which shall be paid in coin, and shall also be lawful money and a legal tender in payment of all debts, public and private, within the United States, except duties on imports and interest as aforesaid.

Holders thereof may deposit any amount not less than $ 50, with the Treasurer or Assistant Treasurer, and receive certificates convertible into United States bonds. And any holders of said United States notes depositing any sum not less than fifty dollars, or some multiple of fifty dollars, with the Treasurer of the United States, or either of the Assistant Treasurers, shall receive in exchange therefor duplicate certificates of deposit, one of which may be transmitted to the Secretary of the Treasury, who shall thereupon issue to the holder an equal amount of bonds of the United States, coupon or registered, as may by said holder be desired, bearing interest at the rate of six per centum per annum, payable semi-annually, and redeemable at the pleasure of the United States after five years, and payable twenty years from the date thereof.

Said notes receivable in payment of loans to the United States. And such United States notes shall be received the same as coin, at their par value, in payment for any loans that may be hereafter sold or negotiated by the Secretary of the Treasury, and may be reissued from time to time as the exigencies of the public interest shall require.

$ 500,000,000 of six-per-cent bonds authorized to fund floating debt. SEC. 2. *And be it further enacted,* That, to enable the Secretary of the Treasury to fund the Treasury-notes and floating debt of the United States, he is hereby authorized to issue, on the credit of the United States, coupon bonds, or registered bonds, to an amount not exceeding five hundred millions of dollars, redeemable at the pleasure of the United States after five years, and payable twenty years

When payable. from date, and bearing interest at the rate of six per centum per annum, payable semi-annually. And the bonds herein authorized shall be of such denominations, Denomination not less than $ 50. not less than fifty dollars, as may be determined upon by the Secretary of the Treasury. And the Secretary of the Treasury may dispose of such bonds at any time, at the May be disposed of for coin or at market value. market value thereof, for the coin of the United States, or for any of the Treasury-notes that have been or may hereafter be issued under any former act of Congress, or for United States notes that may be issued under the provisions of this act ; and all stocks, bonds, and other securities of the United States held by individuals, corporations, or associations, within the United States, shall be exempt Exempt from taxation. from taxation by or under State authority.

SEC. 3. *And be it further enacted,* That the United Form of notes and bonds. States notes and the coupon or registered bonds authorized by this act shall be in such form as the Secretary of the Treasury may direct, and shall bear the written or en- How signed, &c graved signatures of the Treasurer of the United States and the Register of the Treasury, and also, as evidence of lawful issue, the imprint of a copy of the seal of the Treasury Department, which imprint shall be made under the direction of the Secretary, after the said notes or bonds shall be received from the engravers, and before they are issued ; or the said notes and bonds shall be signed by the Treasurer of the United States, or for the Treasurer by such persons as may be specially appointed by the Secretary of the Treasury for that purpose, and shall be countersigned by the Register of the Treasury, or for the Register by such persons as the Secretary of the Treasury may specially appoint for that purpose ; and all the provisions of the act entitled " An Act to authorize the issue of Treasury-notes," approved the twenty-third day of December, eighteen hundred and fifty-seven, so far as they can be applied to this act, and not inconsistent therewith, are hereby revived and re-enacted ; and the sum of three Appropriation of $ 300,000 for expenses of engraving, &c. hundred thousand dollars is hereby appropriated out of any money in the Treasury not otherwise appropriated, to enable the Secretary of the Treasury to carry this act into effect.

SEC. 4. *And be it further enacted,* That the Secretary of the Treasury may receive from any person or persons, or any corporation, United States notes on deposit for not

May be deposited with the United States Treasury in sums of not less than $100, and certificates bearing 5 per cent interest issued therefor. less than thirty days in sums of not less than one hundred dollars, with any of the Assistant Treasurers or designated depositaries of the United States authorized by the Secretary of the Treasury to receive them, who shall issue therefor certificates of deposit, made in such form as the Secretary of the Treasury shall prescribe, and said certificates of deposit shall bear interest at the rate of five per centum per annum, and any amount of United States

Deposits may be withdrawn. notes so deposited may be withdrawn from deposit at any time after ten days' notice on the return of said certificates : *Provided*, That the interest on all such deposits shall cease and determine at the pleasure of the Secretary

Aggregate of deposits not to exceed $ 25,000,000. of the Treasury : *And provided further*, That the aggregate of such deposit shall at no time exceed the amount of twenty-five millions of dollars.

Duties to be received in coin and demand-notes. SEC. 5. *And be it further enacted*, That all duties on imported goods shall be paid in coin, or in notes payable on demand, therefor authorized to be issued, and by law receivable in payment of public dues, and the coin so paid shall be set apart as a special fund, and shall be applied as follows : —

Coin, how used to pay interest. First. To the payment in coin of the interest on the bonds and notes of the United States.

Second. To the purchase or payment of one per centum of the entire debt of the United States, to be made within each fiscal year after the first day of July, eighteen hun-

To create a sinking fund dred and sixty-two, which is to be set apart as a sinking fund, and the interest of which shall in like manner be applied to the purchase or payment of the public debt as the Secretary of the Treasury shall from time to time direct.

Third. The residue thereof to be paid into the Treasury of the United States.

Forging, &c. SEC. 6. *And be it further enacted*, That if any person or persons shall falsely make, forge, counterfeit, or alter, or cause or procure to be falsely made, forged, or counterfeited, or altered, or shall willingly aid or assist in falsely making, forging, counterfeiting, or altering any note, bond, coupon, or other security issued under the authority of this act, or heretofore issued under acts to authorize the issue of Treasury-notes or bonds, or shall pass, alter, publish, or sell, or attempt to pass, alter, publish, or sell, or bring into the United States from any foreign place with intent to pass, alter, publish, or sell, or shall have or keep in possession, or conceal with intent to alter, publish, or sell, any such false, forged, counterfeited, or altered note, bond, coupon, or other security, with intent to defraud any body, corporate or politic, or any other person or persons whatever, every person so offending shall be deemed guilty of felony, and shall, on conviction thereof, be punished by fine not exceeding five thousand dollars, and by imprisonment and confinement to hard labor, not exceeding fifteen years, according to the aggravation of the offence.

How punished.

SEC. 7. *And be it further enacted,* That if any person having the custody of any plate or plates from which any notes, bonds, coupons, or other securities mentioned in this act, or any part thereof, shall have been printed, or which shall have been prepared for the purpose of printing any such notes, bonds, coupons, or other securities, or any part thereof, shall use such plate or plates, or knowingly permit the same to be used for the purpose of printing any notes, bonds, coupons, or other securities, or any part thereof, except such as shall be printed for the use of the United States by order of the proper officer thereof; or if any person shall engrave, or cause or procure to be engraved, or shall aid in engraving any plate or plates in the likeness or similitude of any plate or plates designed for the printing of any such notes, bonds, coupons, or other securities, or any part thereof, or shall vend or sell any such plate or plates, or shall bring into the United States from any foreign place any such plate or plates, with any other intent, or for any purpose, in either case, than that such plate or plates shall be used for printing of such notes, bonds, coupons, or other securities, or some part or parts thereof, for the use of the United States, or shall have in his custody or possession any metallic plate engraved after the similitude of any plate from which any such notes, bonds, coupons, or other securities, or any part or parts thereof, shall have been printed, with intent to use such plate or plates, or cause or suffer the same to be used, in forging or counterfeiting any such notes,

Persons having custody of plates, and using same unlawfully.

Engraving similar plates for fraudulent purposes.

bonds, coupons, or other securities, or any part or parts thereof, issued as aforesaid, or shall have in his custody or possession any blank note or notes, bond or bonds, coupon or coupons, or other security or securities, engraved and printed after the similitude of any notes, bonds, coupons, or other securities, issued as aforesaid, with intent to sell or otherwise use the same; or if any person shall print, photograph, or in any other manner execute, or cause to be printed, photographed, or in any manner executed, or shall aid in printing, photographing, or executing any engraving, photograph, or other print, or impression, in the likeness or similitude of any such notes, bonds, coupons, or other securities, or any part or parts thereof, or shall vend or sell any such engraving, photograph, print, or other impression, except to the United States, or shall bring into the United States from any foreign place any such engraving, photograph, print, or other impression, for the purpose of vending or selling the same, except by the direction of some proper officer of the United States, or shall have in his custody or possession any paper adapted to the making of such notes, bonds, coupons, or other securities, and similar to the paper upon which any such notes, bonds, coupons, or other securities shall have been issued, with intent to use such paper, or cause or suffer the same to be used, in forging or counterfeiting any of the notes, bonds, coupons, or other securities, issued as aforesaid, every person so offending shall be deemed guilty of a felony, and shall, on conviction thereof, be punished by fine not exceeding five thousand dollars, and by imprisonment and confinement to hard labor not exceeding fifteen years, according to the aggravation of the offence.

Fraudulent printing, photographing, &c.

How punished.

Approved February 25, 1862.

AN ACT TO AUTHORIZE THE SECRETARY OF THE TREASURY *March 1, 1862.*
TO ISSUE CERTIFICATES OF INDEBTEDNESS TO PUBLIC
CREDITORS.

Be it enacted by the Senate and House of Representatives of the United States of America in Congress assembled, That the Secretary of the Treasury be, and he is hereby, authorized to cause to be issued to any public creditor, who may be desirous to receive the same upon requisition of the head of the proper Department, in satisfaction of audited and settled demands against the United States, certificates for the whole amount due, or parts thereof, not less than one thousand dollars, signed by the Treasurer of the United States, and countersigned as may be directed by the Secretary of the Treasury ; which certificate shall be payable in one year from date, or earlier, at the option of the government, and shall bear interest at the rate of six per centum per annum.

Issue of certificates of indebtedness authorized.

Not less than $1,000.

How signed.

When payable.

Six per cent interest.

Approved March 1, 1862.

AN ACT TO AUTHORIZE THE PURCHASE OF COIN, AND FOR *March 17, 1862.*
OTHER PURPOSES.

Be it enacted by the Senate and House of Representatives of the United States of America in Congress assembled, That the Secretary of the Treasury may purchase coin with any of the bonds or notes of the United States, authorized by law, at such rates and upon such terms as he may deem most advantageous to the public interest, and may issue, under such rules and regulations as he may prescribe, certificates of indebtedness, such as are authorized by an act entitled " An Act to authorize the Secretary of the Treasury to issue certificates of indebtedness to public creditors," approved March first, eighteen hundred and sixty-two, to such creditors as may desire to receive the same, in discharge of checks drawn by disbursing officers upon sums placed to their credit on the books of the Treasurer, upon requisitions of the proper Departments,

Purchase of coin with any United States bonds or notes authorized.

Certificates of indebtedness may be issued to holders of checks, &c.

as well as in discharge of audited and settled accounts, as provided by said act.

Demand - notes made receivable and a legal tender as notes issued under act of February 25, 1862. SEC. 2. *And be it further enacted,* That the demand-notes, authorized by the act of July seventeenth, eighteen hundred and sixty-one, and by the act of February twelfth, eighteen hundred and sixty-two, shall, in addition to being receivable in payment of duties on imports, be receivable and shall be lawful money and a legal tender, in like manner, and for the same purposes, and to the same extent, as the notes authorized by an act entitled " An Act to authorize the issue of United States notes, and for the redemption or funding thereof, and for funding the floating debt of the United States," approved February twenty-fifth, eighteen hundred and sixty-two.

Secretary of the Treasury authorized to receive deposits of Treasury-notes to amount of $ 50,000,000. SEC. 3. *And be it further enacted,* That the limitation upon temporary deposits of United States notes with any Assistant Treasurers or designated depositaries, authorized by the Secretary of the Treasury to receive such deposits, at five per cent interest, to twenty-five millions of dollars, shall be so far modified as to authorize the Secretary of the Treasury to receive such deposits to an amount not exceeding fifty millions of dollars, and that the rates of interest shall be prescribed by the Secretary of the Treasury, not exceeding the annual rate of five per centum.

May issue new notes in place of those worn out. SEC. 4. *And be it further enacted,* That in all cases where the Secretary of the Treasury is authorized by law to reissue notes, he may replace such as are so mutilated or otherwise injured as to be unfit for use with others of the same character and amount, and such mutilated notes, and all others which by law are required to be taken up and not reissued, shall, when so replaced or taken up, be destroyed in such manner and under such regulations as the Secretary of the Treasury may prescribe.

Approved March 17, 1862.

AN ACT TO AUTHORIZE AN ADDITIONAL ISSUE OF TREASURY- *July 11, 1862.*
NOTES, AND FOR OTHER PURPOSES.

*Be it enacted by the Senate and House of Representatives
of the United States of America in Congress assembled,*
That the Secretary of the Treasury is hereby authorized to
issue, in addition to the amounts heretofore authorized, on
the credit of the United States, one hundred and fifty millions of dollars of United States notes, not bearing interest,
payable to bearer at the Treasury of the United States,
and of such denominations as he may deem expedient:
Provided, That no note shall be issued for the fractional
part of a dollar, and not more than thirty-five millions
shall be of lower denominations than five dollars; and
such notes shall be receivable in payment of all loans made
to the United States, and of all taxes, internal duties, excises, debts, and demands of every kind due to the United
States, except duties on imports and interest, and of all
claims and demands against the United States, except for
interest upon bonds, notes, and certificates of debt or deposit; and shall also be lawful money and a legal tender
in payment of all debts, public and private, within the
United States, except duties on imports and interest, as
aforesaid. And any holder of said United States notes
depositing any sum not less than fifty dollars, or some
multiple of fifty dollars, with the Treasurer of the United
States, or either of the Assistant Treasurers, shall receive
in exchange therefor duplicate certificates of deposit, one
of which may be transmitted to the Secretary of the Treasury, who shall thereupon issue to the holder an equal
amount of bonds of the United States, coupon or registered, as may by said holder be desired, bearing interest at
the rate of six per centum per annum, payable semi-annually, and redeemable at the pleasure of the United
States after five years, and payable twenty years from the
date thereof: *Provided, however,* That any notes issued
under this act may be paid in coin, instead of being received in exchange for certificates of deposit as above specified, at the direction of the Secretary of the Treasury.
And the Secretary of the Treasury may exchange for such

Marginal notes:
Authority to issue $150,000,000 Treasury-notes

$35,000,000 may be of denominations from $1 to $5.

Receivable for all dues except duties on imports and interest on bonds, &c., and convertible into six-per-cent bonds.

May be paid in coin.

notes, on such terms as he shall think most beneficial to
the public interest, any bonds of the United States bearing
six per centum interest, and redeemable after five and
payable in twenty years, which have been or may be lawfully issued under the provisions of any existing act; may
reissue the notes so received in exchange; may receive
and cancel any notes heretofore lawfully issued under any
act of Congress, and in lieu thereof issue an equal amount
in notes such as are authorized by this act; and may purchase, at rates not exceeding that of the current market,

and cost of purchase not exceeding one eighth of one per
centum, any bonds or certificates of debt of the United
States as he may deem advisable.

SEC. 2. *And be it further enacted,* That the Secretary
of the Treasury be, and he is hereby authorized, in case he
shall think it expedient to procure said notes, or any part
thereof, to be engraved and printed by contract, to cause
the said notes or any part thereof to be engraved, printed,
and executed in such form as he shall prescribe, at the
Treasury Department in Washington, and under his direction; and he is hereby empowered to purchase and provide
all the machinery and materials, and to employ such persons and appoint such officers as may be necessary for
this purpose.

SEC. 3. *And be it further enacted,* That the limitation
upon temporary deposits of United States notes with any
Assistant Treasurer or designated Depositary authorized
by the Secretary of the Treasury to receive such deposits
to fifty millions of dollars, be and is hereby repealed; and
the Secretary of the Treasury is authorized to receive such
deposits, under such regulations as he may prescribe, to
such amount as he may deem expedient, not exceeding
one hundred millions of dollars, for not less than thirty
days, in sums not less than one hundred dollars, at a rate
of interest not exceeding five per centum per annum; and
any amount so deposited may be withdrawn from deposit at
any time after ten days' notice, on the return of the certificate of deposit. And of the amounts of United States

notes authorized by this act, not less than fifty millions of
dollars shall be reserved for the purpose of securing prompt
payment of such deposits when demanded, and shall be

issued and used only when, in the judgment of the Secretary of the Treasury, the same or any part thereof, may be needed for that purpose. And certificates of deposit and of indebtedness issued under this or former acts may be received on the same terms as United States notes in payment for bonds redeemable after five and payable in twenty years.

SEC. 4. *And be it further enacted,* That the Secretary of the Treasury may, at any time until otherwise ordered by Congress, and under the restrictions imposed by the "Act to authorize a national loan, and for other purposes," borrow, on the credit of the United States, such part of the sum of two hundred and fifty millions mentioned in said act as may not have been borrowed, under the provisions of the same, within twelve months from the passage thereof.

All certificates of deposit and of indebtedness convertible into bonds.

Time for obtaining loan authorized by act of July 17, 1861, extended.

SEC. 5. *And be it further enacted,* That any part of the appropriation of ten thousand dollars for the detection and bringing to trial of persons engaged in counterfeiting the coin of the United States, made by the act entitled " An Act making appropriations for the legislative, executive, and judicial expenses of the government for the year ending thirtieth of June, eighteen hundred and sixty-one," approved June twenty-three, eighteen hundred and sixty, may be applied in detecting and bringing to trial and punishment persons engaged in counterfeiting Treasury-notes, bonds, or other securities of the United States, as well as the coin of the United States. And to carry into effect the preceding sections of this act, the sum of three hundred thousand dollars is hereby appropriated, out of any money in the Treasury not otherwise appropriated.

Appropriation for punishing counterfeiting of coin, contained in act of June 23, 1860, applied to bonds, notes,&c.,of United States, ch. 205, 1860.

SEC. 6. *And be it further enacted,* That all the provisions of the act entitled " An Act to authorize the issue of United States notes, and for the redemption or funding thereof, and for funding the floating debt of the United States," approved February twenty-five, eighteen hundred and sixty-two, so far as the same can or may be applied to the provisions of this act, and not inconsistent therewith, shall apply to the notes hereby authorized to be issued.

Provisions of act of February 25, 1862, applicable to this act.

Approved July 11, 1862.

ANALYSIS.

Act of 21 July, 1841. — $12,000,000 Six-per-Cent Loan. *July 21, 1841.*

Sec. 1. Authorizes the President of the United States within one year to borrow $12,000,000, or any part thereof, at interest not exceeding six per cent, payable quarterly or semi-annually, to be applied to the redemption of Treasury-notes outstanding, or in the payment of public expenses. Said loan to be reimbursed at the will of the Secretary of the Treasury, after six months' notice, or at any time after 1 January, 1845, and the stock transferable only at the Treasury.

Sec. 2. Requires certificates to be signed by the Secretary, and countersigned by Register of the Treasury, and not to be sold below par.

Sec. 4. Authorizes the Secretary, out of any surplus in Treasury, to purchase said stock at any time before 1 January, 1845.

Sec. 5. Pledges the faith of the United States for punctual payment of interest and principal.

Act of 15 April, 1842. — $17,000,000 (including *April 15, 1842* $12,000,000 authorized by Act of 21 July, 1841) Six-per-Cent Loan.

Sec. 1. Extends the term for borrowing $12,000,000 authorized by act of 21 July, 1841, one year from 15 April, 1842.

Sec. 2. Makes such part of loan as may be obtained after passage of this act reimbursable at the discretion of the Secretary of the Treasury after six months' notice, or at any time within twenty years from 1 January, 1843.

Sec. 3. Certificates to be in form prescribed by the Secretary of Treasury, and transferable by delivery.

Sec. 4. Stock not to be sold below par until proposals have been invited by advertisement for a reasonable time, and then only for the highest price offered. Agent or agents may be appointed to negotiate same, with compensation of one tenth of one per cent on amount negotiated, as authorized by second section of act of 21 July, 1841.

Sec. 5. Pledges receipts from duties on imports, for payment of principal and interest.

Sec. 6. Requires Secretary of Treasury to report to Congress at next session his action under this, and the act of 21 July, 1841.

Sec. 7. Adopts all provisions of act of 21 July, 1841, not hereby changed or modified as part of this act.

Sec. 8. Authorizes the President to borrow $5,000,000 additional under the provisions of the two acts.

Sec. 9. Makes all outstanding Treasury-notes issued under authority of act of 12 October, 1837, and subsequent acts bear interest of six per cent from 5 March, 1842, or from maturity, if they fall due after that time, payable at the Treasury on the first days of January and July, said interest, however, to cease after sixty days' notice of readiness to redeem the said notes.

July 22, 1846. **ACT OF 22 JULY, 1846.—$10,000,000 TREASURY-NOTES, OR SIX-PER-CENT BONDS.**

Sec. 1. Authorizes the President to issue within one year from passage of act $10,000,000 Treasury-notes; and subject to that limit, to issue others in the place of such as may be redeemed, all such emissions to be made under the provisions of the act of 12 October, 1837.

Sec. 2. Authorizes the President, instead of issuing Treasury-notes, to borrow money, and issue therefor stock of the United States, according to the provisions contained in act of 15 April, 1842, redeemable within ten years from time of issue; and provides that the stock and notes issued under this act shall not together exceed the limit of $10,000,000, and that no commission shall be allowed for negotiating the loan.

Sec. 3. Limits interest to be paid on said notes and

stock at six per cent, and forbids the disposition of same below par.

SEC. 5. Appropriates $ 50,000 for reimbursing innocent holders of purloined or stolen notes.

ACT OF 6 AUGUST, 1846. (INDEPENDENT TREASURY ACT.) *August 6, 1846.*

SEC. 18. Authorizes all Treasury-notes issued under authority of the United States to be received in payment of all public dues from and after 1st of January, 1847.

ACT OF 10 AUGUST, 1846. — STOLEN OR PURLOINED TREAS- *August 10, 1846.*
URY-NOTES.

SEC. 1. Authorizes the Secretary, whenever satisfied of the facts by proof taken as therein directed, to pay any innocent holder of Treasury-notes, which have, before the passage of this act, been received or redeemed by any authorized officer of government, and subsequently stolen or purloined, and put into circulation without marks of cancellation, the amount so held.

SEC. 2. Authorizes the Secretary to credit any officer who has in good faith received or paid any such stolen or purloined Treasury-notes with the amount so received or paid.

SEC. 3. Repeals all acts and parts of acts supplied by this act, so far as they have not been acted on, and confirms them so far as they have been acted on.

ACT OF 28 JANUARY, 1847, AUTHORIZING ISSUE OF *January 28, 1847.*
$ 23,000,000 TREASURY-NOTES.

SEC. 1. Authorizes the President to issue $ 23,000,000 Treasury-notes of denominations not less than $ 50.

SEC. 2. Makes said notes redeemable, on presentment at the Treasury, one or two years after date thereof, with interest from date not exceeding six per cent, to be fixed by the Secretary of Treasury, and approved by the President; said interest to cease after sixty days' notice of readiness to redeem, given at any time after maturity of said notes. Faith of the United States pledged for their redemption at the time specified.

SEC. 3. Requires said notes to be signed by the Treasurer of United States, and countersigned by the Register of the Treasury, and a complete record to be kept of all notes issued, and of all redeemed or cancelled.

SEC. 4. Authorizes the Secretary of the Treasury, with the approval of the President, to pay said notes to creditors of the United States, or to borrow money on credit of same, at not less than their par value, including interest.

SEC. 5. Makes notes transferable by delivery, and assignment indorsed thereon.

SECS. 6, 7, 8. Make notes receivable for all public dues, and authorize the Secretary to purchase said notes at par.

SECS. 9, 10, 11. Provide penalties against forging, counterfeiting, &c.; authorize Secretary to make all needful regulations to secure the United States and holders of notes against fraud and losses.

SEC. 12. Authorizes reissue of notes redeemed, within the limit, as to amount, prescribed by this act.

SECS. 13, 14. Authorize holders of all outstanding Treasury-notes to present the same at the Treasury, or other designated agency, and receive therefor six-per-cent funded stock for the principal of said rates, interest to be paid in money; said stock to be transferable on the books of the Treasury, and the United States reserving the right to redeem the same on the 1 of January, 1848, or at any time thereafter.

SEC. 15. Authorizes the issue of $ 5,000,000 of the notes provided for by act of 22 July, 1846, within the time, and subject to the conditions, prescribed by that act.

SEC. 16. Gives the President the discretion to borrow money on six-per-cent stock of United States, instead of issuing Treasury-notes subject to the limit prescribed as to amount; said stock to be redeemable on or after 1 of January, 1848, and not to be disposed of below par.

SEC. 17. Makes all interest on all stock created by this act payable on the first days of January and July.

SEC. 18. Requires each certificate of stock issued under this act to be signed by the Register of the Treasury, and sealed with the seal of the Treasury Department.

SEC. 19. Pledges proceeds of sales of the public lands received after 1 January, 1848, for the redemption of said stock, and directs the Secretary of the Treasury to apply said proceeds, after payment of interest, to the purchase of same at any price not exceeding its par value.

SECS. 20, 21, 22. Provide for expense of issuing notes and stock, — require monthly statement to be published of all notes issued or redeemed, and report to be made at each session of Congress, — limit the time for issue of notes under this act to six months after peace with Mexico.

ACT OF 31 MARCH, 1848. — $16,000,000 SIX-PER-CENT *March* 31, 1848 LOAN.

SECS. 1, 2. Authorize the President to borrow, on the credit of the United States, $16,000,000, interest not to exceed six per cent, payable quarterly or semi-annually ; said stock to be transferable on the books of the Treasury, and redeemable at any time after twenty years from 1 July, 1848 ; the certificates issued for same to be of denominations not less than $50, signed by the Register of the Treasury and sealed with the seal of the Treasury Department, with interest coupons attached when required ; in which case the certificates are to be transferable by delivery, but in no case to be sold below par.

SECS. 3, 4, 5. Require the Secretary of the Treasury, before disposing of said stock, to advertise for proposals for said loan, pledge the faith of the United States to provide for the prompt payment of principal and interest, — authorize payment of same when due out of any unappropriated money in the Treasury, — and appropriate all surplus revenue for the purchase before maturity of any portion of said stock at the market price, if not below par.

SEC. 6. Requires Secretary to report to Congress, at its next session, his action under this law.

March 3, 184.9 ACT of 3 MARCH, 1849, Sec. 3, repeals the proviso to Sec. 19 of act of 28 January, 1847, prohibiting the purchase of the bonds issued under that act at a greater price than par.

Dec. 23, 1857. ACT OF 23 DEC. 1857. — $20,000,000 TREASURY-NOTES.

SECS. 1, 2, 3. Authorize the President to issue $20,000,000 Treasury-notes of denominations not less $100, to be signed by the Treasurer and countersigned by the Register of the Treasury, payable at the Treasury one year from date thereof, and after maturity to bear interest not exceeding six per cent, the rates of interest on the first issue, which shall not exceed $6,000,000, to be fixed by the Secretary of the Treasury and approved by the President. The remaining $14,000,000 shall be sold or exchanged at par for specie, after thirty days' advertisement, at the lowest rate of interest, not exceeding six per cent, which may be bid. When due, interest to cease after sixty days' notice of readiness to redeem ; record to be kept of all notes issued or redeemed or cancelled, and public faith pledged for redemption of notes, principal and interest.

SECS. 4, 5, 6, 7. Authorize the issue of said notes in payment of warrants on the Treasury, the borrowing of money on the credit of the same, the receipt of same at par in payment of all public dues, the transfer of same by assignment indorsed thereon, and delivery thereof; but forbid the issue or disposal of same below par.

SECS. 8, 9, 10. Authorize the Secretary of the Treasury to issue such instructions and regulations in regard to said notes as he may deem best to secure the United States and individuals against loss and fraud, — direct him to pay at maturity said notes, principal and interest, and authorize him to purchase the same at par before maturity, out of any unappropriated money in the Treasury, and also to issue other notes in place of such as may be paid and redeemed ; the power to issue and reissue under this act to cease on 1st January, 1859.

ACT OF 14 JUNE, 1858. — $20,000,000 5-PER-CENT LOAN.

SECS. 1, 2. Authorize the President to borrow, at any time within one year from passage of this act, on the credit of the United States, not exceeding $20,000,000, to be reimbursed at any time after fifteen years from 1st January, 1859; and to issue therefor certificates of stock, not less than $1,000 each, bearing interest not exceeding five per cent, payable semi-annually, with coupons attached, the certificates to be signed by the Register of the Treasury, and sealed with the seal of the Treasury Department, and payable to the lender or his assigns.

SECS. 3, 4. Require the Secretary of the Treasury, before awarding said loan to advertise for proposals for the same, and to make a full report of his proceedings under this act at the next session of Congress; pledge the public faith for the due payment of interest and redemption of principal of said stock, none of which is to be sold below par.

ACT OF 3 MARCH, 1859. — SECTIONS 5 AND 6.

Revive and extend the power of the President to issue and reissue Treasury-notes under the act of 23 December, 1857, to 1 January, 1860, subject to the terms of said act in all respects, except that said notes may be issued bearing interest not exceeding six per cent, and that it shall not be necessary, as required by that act, to exchange them for specie at the lowest rate of interest offered.

The Secretary is authorized to issue, under act of 14 June, 1858, coupon or registered stock, as purchaser may elect.

ACT OF 22 JUNE, 1860. — $21,000,000 LOAN.

SECS. 1, 2. Authorize the President, at any time within twelve months, to borrow $21,000,000 to redeem outstanding Treasury-notes, &c., and for this purpose to issue certificates of stock of no less denomination than $1,000, and payable at a period not less than ten nor more than

9   F *

twenty years, with interest not exceeding six per cent;
said stock to be signed by the Register of the Treasury and
sealed with seal of Treasury Department, and to be transferable at the Treasury, if issued without coupons, but if
issued with coupons attached, to be transferable by delivery.

SECS. 3, 4. Require the Secretary of the Treasury to
advertise for sealed proposals for said loan, and to accept
the best offered by responsible bidders, provided the same
be not below the par value of said stock.

The public faith is pledged for the payment of interest
and principal, and the Secretary is required to report to
Congress his proceedings under this act.

Dec. 17, 1860. ACT OF 17 DECEMBER, 1860. — $10,000,000 TREASURY-
NOTES.

SECS. 1, 2, 3. Authorize the President to issue not exceeding $10,000,000 of Treasury-notes, of denominations
not less than $50, to be signed by the Treasurer, and
countersigned by the Register, and payable at the Treasury one year after date, with six per cent interest from
maturity; but interest on said notes to cease after sixty
days' notice, in one or more papers of Washington, of
readiness to redeem the same. Public faith pledged for
the redemption of said notes.

SECS. 4, 5. Authorize the Secretary of the Treasury,
with the approval of the President, to issue said notes at
par in payment of warrants in favor of such public creditors as will receive them, and also to sell said notes at
par, at the lowest rate of interest which may be offered by
responsible bidders, after advertisement of not less than
ten days in such papers as the President may direct; no
fraction of less than one fourth of one per cent to be considered in deciding on the bids; the said notes to be
assignable by indorsement of the person to whose order
they may be issued.

SECS. 6, 7, 8. Authorize the receipt of said notes in
payment of all public dues of whatever nature, and the
Secretary of the Treasury to make and issue all such rules

and regulations in regard to the same as may be best calculated to promote public convenience and protect the
United States and individuals against fraud and loss.

SECS. 9, 10. Authorize and direct the Secretary of the
Treasury to pay at maturity said notes and interest, and
to purchase the same at par, out of any unappropriated
money in the Treasury, and also to issue other notes in
place of such as may be redeemed and paid; provided the
limit of $10,000,000 above prescribed shall at no time
be exceeded, and that the power to issue and reissue the
same shall cease on the 1st January, 1863.

SECS. 12, 13. Provide against counterfeiting, altering, etc.

SECS. 14, 15. Require the Secretary of the Treasury to
publish monthly statements of notes issued, paid, and redeemed, and of amount outstanding, and direct that all
money obtained under act of 22 June, 1860, shall be used
in the redemption of Treasury-notes issued under this and
former acts.

ACT OF 8 FEBRUARY, 1861. — $25,000,000 LOAN. *February 8, 1861.*

SECS. 1, 2. Authorize the President at any time before
1 July, 1861, to borrow $25,000,000 for redemption of
outstanding Treasury-notes, and to pay current demands
against the Treasury, and for this purpose to cause stock
certificates to be issued (no certificate to be less than
$1,000), payable at a period not less than ten nor more
than twenty years, with interest not exceeding six per
cent, the said stock to be signed by the Register, and sealed
with the seal of the Treasury Department, and if issued
without coupons, to be transferable only at the Treasury,
but if issued with coupons, to be transferable by delivery.

SECS. 3, 4. Require the Secretary of the Treasury, before awarding loan, to advertise for sealed proposals for
same, and report his proceedings minutely to Congress at
its next session. The public faith is pledged for the due
payment of interest and principal.

SECS. 5, 7. Require the residue of loan authorized by
act of 22 June, 1860, as far as may be necessary, applied
to the redemption of Treasury-notes issued under act of

17 December, 1860, and authorize the Secretary of the
Treasury to exchange at par the bonds issued for said
loan for the said Treasury-notes and interest; and also
give him discretion to reject the proposals offered for the
loan herein provided for, and to re-advertise.

ACT OF 2 MARCH, 1861. — $10,000,000 SIX-PER-CENT
LOAN.

SECS. 1, 2. Authorize the President at any time within
twelve months after the passage of this act to borrow
$10,000,000, to be applied to the payment of any appro-
priations made by law (except for the fiscal year ending
30 June, 1861) and of outstanding Treasury-notes, and
to be redeemable at any time after ten years from 1 July,
1861, on giving three months' notice, and at any time
after twenty years without notice, the certificates of stock
to be signed by the Register, and sealed with the seal of
the Treasury Department, and to bear interest not exceeding six per cent, to be transferable only at the Treasury,
if issued without coupons, and if issued with coupons attached, to be transferable by delivery; and no certificates
to be for less than $1,000.

SECS. 3, 4. Require the Secretary of the Treasury to
advertise said loan at least thirty days in the usual form;
and if satisfactory bids for the stock at its par value be not
offered, the President is authorized to issue in lieu thereof,
to the amount limited by this act, Treasury-notes for sums
not less than $50, bearing interest of six per cent, payable
semi-annually on the first days of January and July;
which notes shall be receivable for all public dues, and be
paid, when requested, to public creditors, or exchanged
for coin, at their par value; and similar notes may be
issued in like manner, in lieu of any other loan heretofore
authorized by law, and the holders thereof shall have the
option to exchange the same in sums not less than $500,
for the bonds or stock in lieu of which they were issued.
This authority to issue Treasury-notes to expire on the 30
June, 1862, and said notes to be redeemable at any time
within two years after the passage of this act, and interest

to cease after they have been called in by the Secretary of the Treasury. The public faith is pledged for the payment of all stock and notes issued under this act.

ACT OF 17 JULY, 1861. — $270,000,000 NATIONAL LOAN. *July 17, 1861.*

SECS. 1, 2. Authorize the Secretary of the Treasury, within twelve months, to borrow, on the credit of the United States, not exceeding $250,000,000, by the issue of coupons and registered bonds, or Treasury-notes, in such proportions of each as he may deem best, to be signed by the First and Second Comptroller, or by the Register, and countersigned by such other officers of the Treasury as the Secretary may designate, and all of the denominations of $50 and upwards, to be sealed with the seal of the Treasury Department. The bonds to be redeemable at pleasure after twenty years, and to bear interest not to exceed seven per cent, payable semi-annually ; the registered bonds to be transferable at the Treasury, and the coupon bonds and Treasury-notes by delivery ; the interest coupons to be signed or executed in such manner as the Secretary may designate. Treasury-notes of these classes may be issued as follows, namely : Class 1st, for $50 and upwards, payable three years after date with interest, payable semi-annually, of 7_{10}^{3} per cent. Class 2d, under $50, and not less than $10, payable one year after date with interest 3_{10}^{65} per cent, and exchangeable, in sums not less than $100, for notes of class 1st. Class 3d, under $50, payable on demand without interest, by the Assistant Treasurer at Philadelphia, New York, and Boston ; the issues not bearing interest, not to exceed $50,000,000 ; and all issues of 1st and 2d class may be used in payment of debts or exchanged for coin.

SEC. 3. Requires the Secretary to open books for subscriptions to the Treasury-notes of class 1st, at such places and under such regulations as he may designate, to be superintended by the Assistant Treasurer, and such depositaries, postmasters, and other agents, in the respective places as he may appoint ; notice of the same to be given in two daily newspapers in Washington, and in one or more papers in the several places designated for receiving subscriptions. And if the whole amount subscribed should not be accepted by the Secretary, he shall prefer the smaller subscriptions, and may designate temporary places of deposit for the funds received, until they can be placed in the possession of the official depositaries. But before opening books for subscriptions as above, the Secretary may, if he deem it expedient, use not exceeding $100,000,000 of the notes of class 1st to buy coin, to pay debts, and to redeem Treasury-notes of the issue of 23d December, 1857, falling due 30 June, 1861, on notes issued in exchange for same.

SECS. 4, 5. Require the Secretary, before awarding any of the loan in bonds, as authorized herein, to advertise in usual form for sealed proposals for same in the United States, and authorize him to accept the best proposals made by responsible bidders, if not below par; and he is also authorized to negotiate, not exceeding $100,000,000 of said loan in bonds, in any foreign country, payable at any place in the United States or in Europe, and to appoint agents for the purpose under such regulations as he may make; and the rate of exchange at which the money is received from the lenders shall be the rate at which payment of principal and interest shall be made in Europe.

SEC. 6. Authorizes the Secretary to reissue notes of 2d and 3d class, which may be redeemed, or to issue other notes in their stead to the same amount, but the authority herein to issue and reissue Treasury-notes to expire on 1st January, 1863.

SEC. 7. Authorizes the Secretary to issue not exceeding $20,000,000 additional of Treasury-notes of any of the denominations above specified, payable at twelve months or less time from date, with interest not exceeding six per cent, in exchange for coin or in payment of debts.

SECS. 8 to 11. Require the Secretary to report to next session of Congress his proceedings under this act, pledge the public faith for the payment of all issues under the same, and apply the provisions of the act of 23d December, 1857, to this act, so far as not inconsistent with the same.

ACT OF 5 AUGUST, 1861, supplementary to act of 17 *August i .861.*
July, 1861, authorizes the Secretary to issue six-per-cent
bonds, not less than $500 each, redeemable at pleasure
after twenty years, to the amount of the Treasury-notes,
bearing $7\frac{3}{10}$ per cent interest, issued under said act, and
to exchange them for said notes and interest due thereon ;
and any Treasury-notes payable on demand, authorized by
said act, may be made payable at the depositaries at St.
Louis and Cincinnati, as well as at Philadelphia, New York,
and Boston ; requires all Treasury-notes issued under said
act, or any other acts now in force, to be signed by the
Treasurer, and countersigned by the Register, or for them
by some officer of the Treasury designated by the Secretary ; dispenses with the seal of the Department for said
notes, and authorizes the issue of notes of denominations
not less than $5 ; makes $50,000,000 of demand-notes
receivable for all public dues ; authorizes the Secretary to
deposit any moneys obtained on any loan authorized by
law in any solvent specie-paying bank, and to sell or negotiate for any portion of the loan authorized by act of 17
July, 1861, bonds bearing six per cent interest, payable
semi-annually, at any rate not exceeding seven per cent
interest.

ACT OF 12 FEBRUARY, 1862, authorizes the issue *Feb. 12, 1862*
of $10,000,000 of demand-notes, in addition to the
$50,000,000 authorized by acts of 17 July and 5 August,
1861, and for like purposes, which shall be deemed part
of the loan of $250,000,000, authorized by said act.

ACT OF 25 FEBRUARY, 1862. — $150,000,000 TREASURY- *Feb. 25, 1862.*
NOTES AND $500,000,000 SIX-PER-CENT BONDS.

SEC. 1. Authorizes the Secretary of the Treasury to
issue $150,000,000 of Treasury-notes, payable to bearer
without interest, and of denominations of $5 and up-
wards ; $50,000,000 of said notes to be substituted for a
like amount of demand-notes, as rapidly as the latter can
be taken up. The said notes to be receivable, and a legal

tender, in payment of all debts, public and private, except
duties on imports, and interest on United States bonds
and notes, which must be paid in coin; and also convertible into six-per-cent bonds of the United States, coupon or
registered, redeemable at pleasure after five years, and
payable twenty years after date, in sums not less than $50,
or any multiple of $50, when deposited for that purpose
with the Treasurer, or any Assistant Treasurer, of the
United States. Said notes are also receivable as coin, and
at par value, in payment for all authorized loans, and may
be reissued at the pleasure of the Secretary.

SECS. 2, 3, 4. Authorize the Secretary of the Treasury to
issue not exceeding $500,000,000 of coupon or registered
bonds, of denominations not less than $50, redeemable at
pleasure after five years, and payable twenty years after
date with six per cent interest, payable semi-annually, for
the purpose of funding the Treasury-notes and floating
debt of the United States. And with this view, the
Secretary may dispose of said bonds at any time, at their
market value, for coin of the United States, and for Treasury-notes issued, or which may be issued, under this act.
or any future acts. And all stocks, bonds, and securities
of the United States are exempted from taxation by the
States. The bonds and notes hereby authorized must bear
the written or engraved signatures of the Treasurer and
Register, and also the imprint of a copy of the seal of the
Treasury Department; or they must be signed by the
Treasurer, and countersigned by the Register, or for those
officers, by such persons as the Secretary may designate
for the purpose; and all provisions of the act of 23 December, 1857, not inconsistent with this act, are made
applicable to the same; and the Secretary may receive
United States notes on deposit, in sums not less than
$100, and for not less than thirty days, with any Assistant
Treasurer or other designated depositary, who shall issue
therefor certificates of deposit bearing interest of five per
cent; which deposits may be withdrawn at any time after
ten days' notice and surrender of certificates; the aggregate of said deposits not to exceed $25,000,000, and the
interest to cease at the pleasure of the Secretary.

SEC. 5. Provides that the coin received for duties on

imports shall be applied, first, to the payment of interest
on bonds and notes of the United States, and, secondly, to
the purchase, in each fiscal year after the 1 July, 1862, of
one per cent of the public debt, to be set apart as a sinking
fund; the interest of which fund shall, in like manner, be
applied to the purchase and payment of said debt.

SECS. 6, 7. Provide against forging, counterfeiting, altering, and fraudulent issues of United States bonds and
notes.

ACT OF 1 MARCH, 1862. — SIX-PER-CENT CERTIFICATES OF *March 1, 1862.*
INDEBTEDNESS.

Authorizes the Secretary of the Treasury to issue to
public creditors in satisfaction of audited and settled demands, certificates of indebtedness for not less than
$1,000, signed by the Treasurer, and countersigned as
the Secretary may direct, which shall be payable one year
or less after date, with six per cent interest.

ACT OF 17 MARCH, 1862. — PURCHASE OF COIN, &C. *March 17, 1862.*

Authorizes the Secretary of the Treasury, at his discretion, to purchase coin with any of the bonds or notes of
the United States, and to issue certificates, such as authorized by act of 7 March, 1862, in satisfaction of checks
of disbursing officers on sums to their credit on the books
of the Treasury, as well as in discharge of audited and
settled demands. Makes demand-notes, authorized by
act of 17 July, 1861, and 12 February, 1862, a legal tender to the same extent as the notes authorized by the act
of 25 February, 1862, — extends the limit for receiving
deposits of Treasury-notes, as authorized by act of 25
February, 1862, to $50,000,000, the interest allowed on
same not to exceed five per cent. Authorizes the Secretary
to issue new notes in place of those worn out and mutilated, and requires all notes, taken up and not reissued, to
be destroyed.

10 G

ACT OF 11 JULY, 1862.—$ 150,000,000 OF TREASURY-NOTES.

SECS. 1, 2. Authorize the Secretary of the Treasury to issue, in such form and of such denominations, not less than $ 1, as he may prescribe, $ 150,000,000 of Treasury-notes, not bearing interest, in addition to issues heretofore authorized; but the issue of denominations under $ 5 shall not exceed $ 35,000,000. Said notes are to be receivable in payment of all dues to the United States, except duties on imports and interest, and a legal tender for all debts, public and private, except interest on bonds, notes, certificates of deposit and of indebtedness, issued by the United States, and may also be convertible into any six-per-cent bonds of the United States, coupon or registered, payable after twenty years and redeemable after five years, with interest payable semi-annually, or may be paid in coin, at the discretion of the Secretary, who is authorized to reissue the notes so converted or exchanged. And the Secretary is further authorized to receive and cancel any notes heretofore issued, and replace them with the notes authorized by this act; and also to purchase, at rates not exceeding the current market, such bonds or certificates of debt of the United States as he may deem advisable, the cost of such purchase not to exceed one eighth of one per cent.

SEC. 3. Authorizes the Secretary to receive deposits of Treasury-notes, on the terms and in the manner prescribed in former acts, to an amount not exceeding $ 100,000,000, and requires him to reserve $ 50,000,000 of the notes authorized by this act, for the prompt payment of such deposits and interest. And all certificates of deposit, and of indebtedness, issued under this and former acts, are made receivable as Treasury-notes in payment for bonds, redeemable after five years and payable in twenty years.

SECS. 4, 6. Extend indefinitely the time for the completion of negotiations for the national loan of $ 250,000,000, authorized by act of 17 July, 1861, and make the provisions of the act of 25 February, 1862, so far as not inconsistent with this act, applicable to the notes hereby authorized.

THE LOAN ACT OF 1863.

**An Act to provide ways and means for the support of the Government.
Approved March 3, 1863.**

*Be it enacted by the Senate and House of Representatives of the United
States of America in Congress assembled,* That the Secretary of the
Treasury be, and he is hereby, authorized to borrow, from time to time, on
the credit of the United States, a sum not exceeding three hundred millions of dollars for the current fiscal year, and six hundred millions
for the next fiscal year, and to issue therefor coupon or registered bonds,
payable at the pleasure of the government after such periods as may be
fixed by the Secretary, not less than ten nor more than forty years
from date, in coin, and of such denominations, not less than fifty
dollars, as he may deem expedient, bearing interest at a rate not exceeding six per centum per annum, payable on bonds not exceeding
one hundred dollars, annually, and on all other bonds semi-annually, in
coin ; and he may in his discretion dispose of such bonds at any time,
upon such terms as he may deem most advisable, for lawful money
of the United States, or for any of the certificates of indebtedness or
deposit that may at any time be unpaid, or for any of the Treasury notes
heretofore issued or which may be issued under the provisions of this
act.   And all the bonds and Treasury notes or United States notes issued
under the provisions of this act shall be exempt from taxation by or under State or municipal authority : *Provided,* That there shall be outstanding of bonds, Treasury notes, and United States notes, at any time,
issued under the provisions of this act, no greater amount altogether than
the sum of nine hundred millions of dollars.

Sec. 2. *And be it further enacted,* That the Secretary of the Treasury
be, and he is hereby, authorized to issue, on the credit of the United
States, four hundred millions of dollars in Treasury notes, payable at the

pleasure of the United States, or at such time or times not exceeding
three years from date as may be found most beneficial to the public in-
terests, and bearing interest at a rate not exceeding six per centum per
annum, payable at periods expressed on the face of said Treasury notes;
and the interest on the said Treasury notes and on certificates of indebtedness and deposit hereafter issued shall be paid in lawful money.   The
Treasury notes thus issued shall be of such denomination as the Secretary may direct, not less than ten dollars, and may be disposed of on
the best terms that can be obtained, or may be paid to any creditor of
the United States willing to receive the same at par.   And said Treasury
notes may be made a legal tender to the same extent as United States
notes, for their face value, excluding interest; or they may be made exchangeable under regulations prescribed by the Secretary of the Treasury, by the holder thereof at the Treasury in the city of Washington, or
at the office of any Assistant Treasurer or depositary designated for that
purpose, for United States notes equal in amount to the Treasury notes offered for exchange, together with the interest accrued and due thereon at the
date of interest payment next preceding such exchange.   And in lieu of
any amount of said Treasury notes thus exchanged, or redeemed, or paid
at maturity, the Secretary may issue an equal amount of other Treasury
notes; and the Treasury notes so exchanged, redeemed, or paid, shall
be cancelled and destroyed as the Secretary may direct.   In order
to secure certain and prompt exchanges of United States notes for
Treasury notes, when required as above provided, the Secretary shall
have power to issue United States notes to the amount of one hundred
and fifty millions of dollars, which may be used if necessary for such exchanges; but no part of the United States notes authorized by this section shall be issued for or applied to any other purposes than said exchanges; and whenever any amount shall have been so issued and applied, the same shall be replaced as soon as practicable from the sales of
Treasury notes for United States notes.

SEC. 3. *And be it further enacted,* That the Secretary of the Treasury
be, and he is hereby, authorized, if required by the exigencies of the public service, for the payment of the army and navy, and other creditors of
the government, to issue on the credit of the United States the sum of
one hundred and fifty millions of dollars of United States notes, including the amount of such notes heretofore authorized by the joint resolution approved January seventeen, eighteen hundred and sixty-three, in
such form as he may deem expedient, not bearing interest, payable to
bearer, and of such denominations, not less than one dollar, as he may

prescribe, which notes so issued shall be lawful money and a legal tender in payment of all debts, public and private, within the United States, except for duties on imports and interest on the public debt; and any of the said notes, when returned to the Treasury, may be re-issued from time to time as the exigencies of the public service may require. And in lieu of any of said notes, or any other United States notes, returned to the Treasury, and cancelled or destroyed, there may be issued equal amounts of United States notes, such as are authorized by this act. And so much of the act to authorize the issue of United States notes, and for other purposes, approved February twenty-five, eighteen hundred and sixty-two, and of the act to authorize an additional issue of United States notes, and for other purposes, approved July eleven, eighteen hundred and sixty-two, as restricts the negotiation of bonds to market value, is hereby repealed. And the holders of United States notes, issued under and by virtue of said acts, shall present the same for the purpose of exchanging the same for bonds, as therein provided, on or before the first day of July, eighteen hundred and sixty-three, and thereafter the right so to exchange the same shall cease and determine.

SEC. 4. *And be it further enacted,* That in lieu of postage and revenue stamps for fractional currency, and of fractional notes, commonly called postage currency, issued or to be issued, the Secretary of the Treasury may issue fractional notes of like amounts in such form as he may deem expedient, and may provide for the engraving, preparation, and issue thereof, in the Treasury Department building. And all such notes issued shall be exchangeable by the Assistant Treasurers and designated depositaries for United States notes, in sums not less than three dollars, and shall be receivable for postage and revenue stamps, and also in payment of any dues to the United States less than five dollars, except duties on imports, and shall be redeemed on presentation at the Treasury of the United States in such sums and under, such regulations as the Secretary of the Treasury shall prescribe : *Provided,* That the whole amount of fractional currency issued, including postage and revenue stamps issued as currency, shall not exceed fifty millions of dollars.

SEC. 5. *And be it further enacted,* That the Secretary of the Treasury is hereby authorized to receive deposits of gold coin and bullion with the Treasurer or any Assistant Treasurer of the United States, in sums not less than twenty dollars, and to issue certificates therefor in denominations of not less than twenty dollars each, corresponding with the denominations of the United States notes. The coin and bullion deposited for or representing the certificates of deposit shall be retained in the

Treasury for the payment of the same on demand. And certificates representing coin in the Treasury may be issued in payment of interest on the public debt, which certificates, together with those issued for coin and bullion deposited, shall not at any time exceed twenty per centum beyond the amount of coin and bullion in the Treasury ; and the certificates for coin or bullion in the Treasury shall be received at par in payment for duties on imports.

SEC. 6. *And be it further enacted,* That the coupon or registered bonds, Treasury notes, and United States notes authorized by this act, shall be in such form as the Secretary of the Treasury may direct, and shall have printed upon them such statements, showing the amount of accrued or accruing interest, the character of the notes, and the penalties or punishment for altering or counterfeiting them, as the Secretary of the Treasury may prescribe, and shall bear the written or engraved signatures of the Treasurer of the United States and the Register of the Treasury, and also, as evidence of lawful issue, the imprint of the copy of the seal of the Treasury Department, which imprint shall be made, under the direction of the Secretary, after the said notes or bonds shall be received from the engravers and before they are issued ; or the said notes and bonds shall be signed by the Treasurer of the United States, or for the Treasurer by such persons as may be specially appointed by the Secretary of the Treasury for that purpose, and shall be countersigned by the Register of the Treasury, or for the Register by such persons as the Secretary of the Treasury may specially appoint for that purpose. And all the provisions of the act entitled " An act to authorize the issue of Treasury notes," approved the twenty-third day of December, eighteen hundred and fifty-seven, so far as they can be applied to this act, and not inconsistent therewith, are hereby revived and re-enacted.

SEC. 7. *And be it further enacted,* That all banks, associations, corporations or individuals, issuing notes or bills for circulation as currency, shall be subject to and pay a duty of one per centum each half year from and after April first, eighteen hundred and sixty-three, upon the average amount of circulation of notes or bills as currency issued beyond the amoun thereinafter named ;—that is to say, banks, associations, corporations or individuals having a capital of not over one hundred thousand dollars, ninety per centum thereof ; over one hundred thousand and not over two hundred thousand dollars, eighty per centum thereof ; over two hundred thousand and not over three hundred thousand dollars, seventy per centum thereof ; over three hundred thousand and not over five hundred thousand dollars, sixty per centum thereof ; over five hundred thousand and not over one million of dollars, fifty per centum thereof; over one million and not over one million and a half of dollars, forty per centum thereof; over one million and a half, and not over two millions of dollars, thirty per centum thereof; over two millions of dollars, twenty-five per centum thereof. In the case of banks with branches, the duty herein provided for shall be imposed upon the circulation of the notes or bills of such branches severally, and not upon the aggregate circulation of all; and the amount of capital of each branch shall be considered to be the amount allotted to or used by such branch : and all such banks, associations, corporations and individuals shall also be subject to and pay a duty of one-half of one per centum each half year from and after April first, eighteen hundred and sixty-three, upon the average amount of notes or bills not otherwise herein taxed and outstanding as currency during the six months next preceding the return hereinafter provided for ; and the rates of tax or duty imposed on the circulation of associations which may be organized under the act " to provide a national currency secured by a pledge of United States stocks, and to provide for the circulation and redemption thereof," approved February twenty-fifth, eighteen hundred and sixty-three, shall be the same as that hereby imposed on the circulation and deposits of all banks, associations, corporations or individuals, but shall be assessed and collected as required by said act. All banks, associations or corporations and individuals issuing or re-issuing notes or bills for circulation as currency after April first, eighteen hundred and sixty-three, in sums representing any fractional part of a dollar, shall be subject to and pay a duty of five per centum each half year thereafter upon the amount of such fractional notes or bills so issued. And all banks, associations, corporations and individuals receiving deposits of money subject to payment on check or draft, except savings institutions, shall be subject to a duty of one-eighth of one per centum each half year from and after April first, eighteen hundred and sixty-three, upon the average amount of such deposits beyond the average amount of their circulating notes or bills lawfully issued and outstanding as currency. And a list or return shall be made and rendered within thirty days after the first day of October, eighteen hundred and sixty-three, and each six months thereafter, to the Commissioner of Internal Revenue, which shall contain a true and faithful account of the amount of duties accrued, or which should accrue, on the full amount of the fractional note circulation and on the average amount of all other circulation and of all such deposits for the six months next preceding. And there shall be annexed to every such list or return a declaration, under oath or affirmation, to be made in form and manner as shall be prescribed

by the Commissioner of Internal Revenue, of the president, or some other
proper officer of said bank, association, corporation or individual, respectively, that the same contains a true and faithful account of the duties
which have accrued, or which should accrue, and not accounted for; and
for any default in the delivery of such list or return, with such declaration
annexed, the bank, association, corporation, or individual making such
default, shall forfeit, as a penalty, the sum of five hundred dollars
And such bank, association, corporation, or individual shall, upon ren-
dering the list or return as aforesaid, pay to the Commissioner of Internal Revenue the amount of the duties due on such list or return, and
in default thereof shall forfeit, as a penalty, the sum of five hundred dollars; and in case of neglect or refusal to make such list or return as
aforesaid, or to pay the duties as aforesaid, for the space of thirty days
after the time when said list should have been made or rendered, or when
said duties shall have become due and payable, the assessment and collection shall be made according to the general provisions prescribed in
an act entitled "An act to provide internal revenue to support the government and to pay interest on the public debt," approved July one,
eighteen hundred and sixty-two.

SEC. 8. *And be it further enacted*, That in order to prevent and punish
counterfeiting and fraudulent alterations of the bonds, notes and fractional
currency authorized to be issued by this act, all the provisions of the
sixth and seventh sections of the act entitled "An act to authorize the
issue of United States notes, and for the redemption or funding thereof,
and for funding the floating debt of the United States," approved February twenty-fifth, eighteen hundred and sixty-two, shall, so far as applicable, apply to the bonds, notes, and fractional currency hereby authorized
to be issued, in like manner as if the said sixth and seventh sections were
hereby adopted as additional sections of this act. And the provisions
and penalties of said sixth and seventh sections shall extend and apply to
all persons who shall imitate, counterfeit, make, or sell any paper such as
that used, or provided to be used, for the fractional notes prepared, or to
be prepared, in the Treasury Department building, and to all officials of
the Treasury Department engaged in engraving and preparing the bonds,
notes, and fractional currency hereby authorized to be issued, and to all
official and unofficial persons in any manner employed under the provisions of this act. And the sum of six hundred thousand dollars is hereby
appropriated, out of any money in the Treasury not otherwise appropriated, to enable the Secretary of the Treasury to carry this act into
effect.

Approved March 3, 1863.

'

THE LOAN ACTS OF 1864.

I. *The Ten-Forty Act of March*, 1864.　II. *The Four Hundred Million*. *Act of June,* 1864.　III. *The Special Income Tax Law.*　IV. *The Patriotic Loan of* 1864.

TEN-FORTY LOAN OF THE UNITED STATES.

An Act supplementary to an Act, entitled " An Act to provide Ways and Means for the support of the Government," approved March third, eighteen hundred and sixty-three.

Be it enacted by the Senate and House of Representatives of the United States of America, in Congress assembled, That in lieu of so much of the loan authorized by the act of March third, eighteen hundred and sixty-three, to which this is supplementary, the Secretary of the Treasury is authorized to borrow, from time to time, on the credit of the United States, not exceeding two hundred millions of dollars during the current fiscal year, and to prepare and issue therefor coupon or registered bonds of the United States, bearing date March first, eighteen hundred and sixty-four, or any subsequent period, redeemable at the pleasure of the government after any period not less than five years, and payable at any period not more than forty years from date, in coin, and of such denomi-. nations as may be found expedient, not less than fifty dollars, bearing interest not exceeding six per centum a year, payable on bonds not over one hundred dollars, annually, and on all other bonds semi-annually, in coin : and he may dispose of such bonds at any time, on such terms as he may deem most advisable, for lawful money of the United States ; or, at his discretion, for Treasury notes, certificates of indebtedness, or certificates of deposit, issued under any act of Congress ; and all bonds issued under this act shall be exempt from taxation by or under State or municipal authority.　And the Secretary of the Treasury shall pay the necessary expenses of the preparation, issue and disposal of such bonds out of any money in the Treasury not otherwise appropriated, but the amount so paid shall not exceed one-half of one per centum of the amount of the bond so issued and disposed of.

SEC. 2. *And be it further enacted,* That the Secretary of the Treasury is hereby authorized to issue to persons who subscribed on or before the twenty-first day of January, eighteen hundred and sixty-four, for bonds redeemable, after five years, and payable twenty years from date, and have paid into the Treasury the amount of their subscriptions, the bonds

by them respectively subscribed for, not exceeding eleven millions of
dollars; notwithstanding that such subscriptions may be in excess of five
hundred millions of dollars; and the bonds so issued shall have the same
force and effect as if issued under the provisions of the act "to authorize
the issue of United States notes and for other purposes," approved February twenty-sixth, eighteen hundred and sixty-two.

Approved March 3, 1864.

II. Act authorizing a Loan of Four Hundred Millions of Dollars. Approved June 30, 1864.

An Act to provide Ways and Means for the support of the Government and for other purposes.

Be it enacted by the Senate and House of Representatives of the United States of America, in Congress assembled, That the Secretary of the Treasury be, and he is hereby authorized to borrow, from time to time, on the credit of the United States, four hundred millions of dollars, and to issue therefor coupon or registered bonds of the United States, re-deemable at the pleasure of the government, after any period not less than five nor more than thirty years, or, if deemed expedient, made pay-able at any period not more than forty years from date. And said bonds shall be of such denominations as the Secretary of the Treasury shall direct, not less than fifty dollars, and bear an annual interest not exceed-ing six per centum, payable semi-annually in coin. And the Secretary of the Treasury may dispose of such bonds, or any part thereof, and of any bonds commonly known as five-twenties remaining unsold, in the United States, or if he shall find it expedient, in Europe, at any time, on such terms as he may deem most advisable, for lawful money of the United States, or, at his discretion, for Treasury notes, certificates of in-debtedness, or certificates of deposit issued under any act of Congress. And all bonds, Treasury notes, and other obligations of the United States, shall be exempt from taxation by or under State or municipal authority.

Sec. 2. *And be it further enacted,* That the Secretary of the Treasury may issue on the credit of the United States, and in lieu of an equal amount of bonds authorized by the preceding section, and as a part of said loan, not exceeding two hundred millions of dollars, in Treasury notes of any denomination not less than ten dollars, payable at any time not exceeding three years from date; or, if thought more expedient, re-deemable at any time after three years from date, and bearing interest not exceeding the rate of seven and three-tenths per centum, payable in lawful money at maturity, or, at the discretion of the Secretary, semi-annually. And the said Treasury notes may be disposed of by the Sec-retary of the Treasury on the best terms that can be obtained, for law-ful money; and such of them as shall be made payable, principal and interest, at maturity, shall be a legal tender to the same extent as United States notes for their face value, excluding interest, and may be paid to any creditor of the United States at their face value, excluding interest or to any creditor willing to receive them at par, including interest; and any Treasury notes issued under the authority of this act may be made convertible, at the discretion of the Secretary of the Treasury, into any bonds issued under the authority of this act. And the Secretary of the Treasury may redeem and cause to be cancelled and destroyed any Treasury notes or United States notes heretofore issued under authority of previous acts of Congress, and substitute, in lieu thereof, an equal amount of Treasury notes such as are authorized by this act, or of other United States notes: *Provided,* That the total amount of bonds and Treasury, notes authorized by the first and second sections of this act shall not exceed four hundred millions of dollars, in addition to the amounts heretofore issued; nor shall the total amount of United States notes, issued or to be issued, ever exceed four hundred millions of dollars, and such additional sum, not exceeding fifty millions of dollars, as may be temporarily required for the redemption of temporary loans; nor shall any Treasury note bearing interest, issued under this act, be a legal tender in payment or redemption of any notes issued by any bank, banking association, or banker, calculated or intended to circulate as money.

SEC. 3. *And be it further enacted,* That the interest on all bonds heretofore issued, payable annually, may be paid semi-annually; and in lieu of such bonds authorized to be issued, the Secretary of the Treasury may issue bonds bearing interest, payable semi-annually. And he may also issue, in exchange for Treasury notes heretofore issued, bearing seven and three-tenths per centum interest, besides the six per centum bonds heretofore authorized, like bonds of all the denominations in which such Treasury notes have been issued; and the interest on such Treasury notes after maturity shall be paid in lawful money, and they may be exchanged for such bonds at any time within three months from the date of notice of redemption by the Secretary of the Treasury, after which the interest on such Treasury notes shall cease. And so much of the law approved March third, eighteen hundred and sixty-four, as limits the loan authorized therein to the current fiscal year, is hereby repealed; and the authority of the Secretary of the Treasury to borrow money and issue therefor bonds or notes, conferred by the first section of the act of March third, eighteen hundred and sixty-three, entitled "An act to provide ways and means for the support of the government," shall cease on and after the passage of this act, except so far as it may effect [affect] seventy-five millions of bonds already advertised.

SEC. 4. *And be it further enacted,* That the Secretary of the Treasury may authorize the receipt, as a temporary loan, of United States notes, or the notes of national banking associations on deposit for not less than thirty days, in sums of not less than fifty dollars, by any of the assistant treasurers of the United States, or depositories designated for that purpose, other than national banking associations, who shall issue certificates of deposit in such form as the Secretary of the Treasury shall prescribe, bearing interest not exceeding six per centum annually, and payable at any time after the term of deposit, and after ten days' subsequent notice, unless time and notice be waived by the Secretary of the Treasury; and the Secretary of the Treasury may increase the interest on deposits at less than six per centum to that rate, or, on ten days' notice to depositors, may diminish the rate of interest as the public interest may require; but the aggregate of such deposits shall not exceed one hundred and fifty millions of dollars; and the Secretary of the Treasury may issue, and shall hold in reserve for payment of such deposits, United States notes, not exceeding fifty millions of dollars, including the amount already applied in such payment; and the United States notes, so held in reserve, shall be used only when needed, in his judgment, for the prompt payment of such deposits on demand, and shall be withdrawn and placed again in reserve as the amount of deposits shall again increase.

Sec. 5. *And be it further enacted*, That the Secretary of the Treasury may issue notes of the fractions of a dollar as now used for currency, in such form, with such inscriptions, and with such safeguards against counterfeiting, as he may judge best, and provide for the engraving and preparation, and for the issue of the same, as well as of all other notes and bonds, and other obligations, and shall make such regulations for the redemption of said fractional notes and other notes when mutilated or defaced, and for the receipt of said fractional notes in payment of debts to the United States, except for customs, in such sums, not over five dollars, as may appear to him expedient; and it is hereby declared, that all laws and parts of laws applicable to fractional notes engraved and issued as herein authorized, apply equally and with like force to all the fractional notes heretofore authorized, whether known as postage currency or otherwise, and to postage stamps issued as currency; but the whole amount of all descriptions of notes or stamps less than one dollar issued as currency, shall not exceed fifty millions of dollars.

Sec. 6. *And be it further enacted*, That the coupon and registered bonds shall be in such form and bear such inscriptions as the Secretary of the Treasury may direct, and shall be signed by the Register of the Treasury, or for the Register, by such person or persons as may be specially designated for that purpose by the Secretary of the Treasury, and shall bear, as evidence of lawful issue, the imprint of the seal of the Treasury Department, to be made under the direction of the Secretary of the Treasury, in a room set apart especially and exclusively for that purpose, under the care of some person appointed directly by him. And the coupons attached to such bonds shall bear the engraved signature of the Register of the Treasury, and such other device or safeguard against counterfeiting as the Secretary may approve; and it is hereby declared that all bonds heretofore issued, bearing the signature of the Register, shall have the same force, effect and validity as if signed also by the Treasurer; and all bonds bearing the signature of the Register, erroneously described as Treasurer of the United States, shall have the same force, effect and validity as if his official designation had been correctly stated; and all coupons bearing the engraved signature of the Register of the Treasury in office at the time when such signatures were authorized and engraved, shall have full force, validity and effect, notwithstanding such Register may have subsequently ceased to hold office as such, when issued in connection with bonds duly authorized and signed by or for the successor or successors of said Register. And the Treasury notes and United States notes authorized by this act shall be in such form as the

Secretary of the Treasury shall direct, and shall bear the written or engraved signatures of the Treasurer of the United States and the Register of the Treasury, and shall have printed upon them such statements, showing the amount of accrued or accruing interest and the character of the notes, as the Secretary of the Treasury may prescribe; and shall bear as a further evidence of lawful issue, the imprint of the seal of the Treasury Department, to be made under the direction of the Secretary of the Treasury, as before directed.

SEC. 7. *And be it further enacted,* That the Secretary of the Treasury is hereby authorized to issue, upon such terms and under such regulations as he may from time to time prescribe, registered bonds in exchange for, and in lieu of, any coupon bonds which have been or may hereafter be lawfully issued; such registered bonds to be similar in all respects to the registered bonds issued under the acts authorizing the issue of the coupon bonds offered for exchange. And for all mutilated, defaced, or endorsed coupon or other bonds presented to the Department, the Secretary of the Treasury is authorized to issue, upon terms and under regulations as aforesaid, and in substitution therefor, other bonds of like or equivalent issues.

SEC. 8. *And be it further enacted,* That the Secretary of the Treasury is hereby authorized and required to make and issue, from time to time, such instructions, rules and regulations, to the several collectors, receivers, depositories, officers and others, who may receive Treasury notes, United States notes, or other securities in behalf of the United States, or who may be in any way engaged or employed in the preparation and issue of the same, as he shall deem best calculated to promote the public convenience and security, and to protect the United States as well as individuals from fraud or loss.

SEC. 9. *And be it further enacted,* That the necessary expenses of engraving, printing, preparing and issuing the United States notes, Treasury notes, fractional notes and bonds, hereby authorized, and of disposing of the same to subscribers and purchasers, shall be paid out of any money in the Treasury not otherwise appropriated; but the whole amount thereof shall not exceed one per centum on the amount of notes and bonds issued.

SEC. 10. *And be it further enacted,* That if any person or persons shall falsely make, forge, counterfeit or alter, or cause or procure to be falsely made, forged, counterfeited or altered, any obligation or security of the United States, or shall pass, utter, publish or sell, or attempt to pass, utter, publish or sell, or shall bring into the United States from any foreign place with intent to pass, utter, publish or sell, or shall have or keep in possession or conceal, with intent to utter, publish or sell any such false, forged, counterfeited or altered obligation, or other security, with intent to deceive or defraud, or shall knowingly aid or assist in any of the acts aforesaid, every person so offending shall be deemed guilty of felony, and shall, on conviction thereof, be punished by fine not exceeding five thousand dollars, and by imprisonment and confinement at hard labor not exceeding fifteen years, according to the aggravation of the offence.

SEC. 11. *And be it further enacted,* That if any person having control, custody or possession of any plate or plates from which any obligation or other security, or any part thereof, shall have been printed, or which may have been prepared by direction from the Secretary of the Treasury, for the purpose of printing any such obligation or other security, or any part thereof, shall use such plate or plates,. or knowingly suffer the same to be used for the purpose of printing any such or similar obligation or other security, or any part thereof, except such as shall be printed for the use of the United States, by order of the proper officer thereof; or, if any person shall engrave, or cause or procure to be engraved, or shall aid or assist in engraving, any plate or plates in the likeness or similitude of any plate or plates designed for the printing of any such obligation or other security, or any part thereof, or shall vend or sell any such plate or plates, or shall bring into the United States from any foreign place any such plate or plates, except under the direction of the Secretary of the Treasury or other proper officer, or with any other intent, or for any other purpose, in either case than that such plate or plates shall be used for the printing of such notes, bonds, coupons or other obligations or securities, or some part or parts thereof, for the use of the United States, or shall have in his control, custody or possession, any metallic plate engraved after the similitude of any plate from which any such obligation or other security, or any part or parts thereof, shall have been printed, with intent to use such plate or plates, or cause or suffer the same to be used in forging or counterfeiting any such obligation or other security, or any part or parts thereof, or shall have in his custody or possession, except under authority from the Secretary of the Treasury or other proper officer, any obligation or other security, engraved and printed after the similitude of any obligation or other security issued under the authority of the United States, with intent to sell or otherwise use the same; or, if any person shall print, photograph, or in any other manner make or execute, or cause to be printed, photographed, or in any manner made or executed, or shall aid in printing, photographing, making or executing any engraving, photograph or other print or impression in the likeness or similitude of any obligation or other security, or any part or parts thereof, or shall vend or sell any such engraving, photograph, print or other impression, except to the United States, or shall bring into the United States from any foreign place any such engraving, photograph, print or other impression, except by the direction of some proper officer of the United States, or shall have or retain in his custody or possession, after a distinctive paper shall have been adopted by the Secretary of the Treasury for obligations and other securities of the United States, any similar paper adapted to the making of any such obligation or other security, except under authority of the Secretary of the Treasury or some other proper officer of the United States, every person so offending shall be deemed guilty of a felony, and shall, on conviction thereof, be punished by fine not exceeding five thousand dollars, or by imprisonment and confined at hard labor, not exceeding fifteen years, or by both, in the discretion of the court.

SEC. 12. *And be it further enacted,* That if any person shall have or retain in his or her custody, possession or contro., without the written authority or warrant of the Secretary of the Treasury, or of the Comptroller of the Currency, approved by the Secretary of the Treasury, any engraved or transferred plate, block or electrotype, or any die, roll or other original work used in making or preparing any plate, block or electrotype, or any plate, block or electrotype prepared or made after the similitude of any plate, block or electrotype from which any obligation or other security authorized to be issued by any act of Congress, or any part thereof, has been or may hereafter be printed, or shall use, or cause or knowingly suffer the same to be used, in forging or counterfeiting any such obligation or other security, or shall print, or cause to be printed, any bronzed or gilt letters or devices, or shall print, or cause to be printed, any letters, figures or devices with green ink, or any green color or pigment upon any note, bond or other representative of value intended or adapted to be used as a currency or a circulating medium, every such person, being thereof convicted, by due course of law, shall be deemed guilty of felony, and shall be imprisoned and kept at hard labor for a term not more than ten years, and fined in a sum not more than ten thousand dollars: *Provided,* That nothing in this act shall affect any prosecution pending, or any civil or criminal liabilities incurred under any former act: *Provided, further,* That the foregoing provisions of this section shall not be held or construed to deprive any person of the right to retain in his custody and possession and use, for any lawful purpose, any engraved or transferred plate, block or electrotype, or any die, roll or other original work as aforesaid, which had been used by him in printing or engraving bank notes or other obligations before being used in printing any obligation or other security authorized to be issued by any act of Congress; nor shall any of said foregoing provisions be held or construed to prohibit or restrain the lawful use by any person of any ink, color or pigment, the exclusive right to which has been secured to any such person by letters patent which are still in force.

Sec. 13. *And be it further enacted,* That the words " obligation or other security of the United States," used in this act, shall be held to include and mean all bonds, coupons, national currency, United States notes, Treasury notes, fractional notes, checks for money of authorized officers of the United States, certificates of indebtedness, certificates of deposit, stamps and other representatives of value, of whatever denomination, which have been or may be issued under any act of Congress.

Approved June 30, 1864.

———

III. The Special Income Tax.

Joint Resolution imposing a Special Income Duty.

Resolved, by the Senate and House of Representatives of the United States of America, in Congress assembled, That in addition to the income duty already imposed by law, there shall be levied, assessed and collected, on the first day of October, eighteen hundred and sixty-four, a

special income duty upon the gains, profits or income for the year ending the thirty-first day of December, and preceding the time herein
named, by levying, assessing, and collecting said duty of all persons re-
siding within the United States, or of citizens of the United States resid-
ing abroad, at the rate of five per centum on all sums exceeding six hundred dollars, and that the same be levied, assessed, estimated and collected, except as to the rate, according to the provisions of existing laws
for the collection of an income duty, annually, when not inapplicable
hereto ; and the Secretary of the Treasury is hereby authorized to make
such rules and regulations as to the time and mode, or other matters, to
enforce the collection of the special income duty herein provided for, as
may be necessary : *Provided,* That in estimating the annual gains, profits or income as aforesaid, for the foregoing special income duty, no de-
ductions shall be made for dividends or interest received from any association, corporation or company, nor shall any deduction be made for any
salary or pay received.

Approved July 4th, 1864.

IV: The Patriotic Loan of 1864.

*Address of the Secretary of the Treasury to the People of the United
States.*

TREASURY DEPARTMENT, *July* 25, 1864.

By an act of Congress, approved June 30, 1864, the Secretary of the
Treasury is authorized to issue an amount not exceeding two hundred
millions of dollars in Treasury notes, bearing interest at a rate not exceeding seven and three-tenths per centum, redeemable after three years
from date, and to exchange the same for lawful money. The Secretary
is further authorized to convert the same into bonds, bearing interest at
a rate not exceeding six per centum, payable in coin. In pursuance of
the authority thus conferred, I now offer to the people of the United
States Treasury notes as described in my advertisement, dated July 25,
1864.

The circumstances under which this loan is asked for, and your aid
invoked, though differing widely from the existing state of affairs three
years ago, are such as to afford equal encouragement and security. Time,
while proving that the struggle for national unity was to exceed in dura-
tion and severity our worst anticipations, has tested the national strength,
and developed the national resources, to an extent alike unexpected and
remarkable, exciting equal astonishment at home and abroad. Three
years of war have burdened you with a debt which, but three years since,
would have seemed beyond your ability to meet. Yet the accumulated
wealth and productive energies of the nation have proved to be so vast,
that it has been borne with comparative ease, and a peaceful future would
hardly feel its weight. As a price paid for national existence, and the
preservation of free institutions, it does not deserve a moment's consideration.

Thus far the war has been supported and carried on, as it only could have been, by a people resolved, at whatever cost of blood and treasure, to transmit, unimpaired, to posterity, the system of free government bequeathed to them by the great men who framed it. This deliberate and patriotic resolve has developed a power surprising even to themselves. It has shown that in less than a century a nation has arisen, unsurpassed in vigor, and exhaustless in resources, able to conduct, through a series of years, war on its most gigantic scale; and finding itself, when near its close, almost unimpaired in all the material elements of power. It has, at the present moment, great armies in the field, facing an enemy v pparently approaching a period of utter exhaustion, but still struggling with a force the greater and more desperate, as it sees, and because it sees, the near approach of a final and fatal consummation. Such, in my deliberate judgment, is the present condition of the great contest for civil liberty in which you are now engaged.

Up to the present moment you have readily and cheerfully afforded the means necessary to support your government in this protracted struggle. It is *your* war. You proclaimed it, and you have sustained it against traitors everywhere, with a patriotic devotion unsurpassed in the world's history.

The securities offered are such as should command your ready confidence. Much effort has been made to shake public faith in our national credit, both at home and abroad. As yet we have asked no foreign aid. Calm and self-reliant, our own means have thus far proved adequate to our wants. They are yet ample to meet those of the present and the future. It still remains for a patriotic people to furnish the needful supply. The brave men who are fighting our battles by land and sea must be fed and clothed, munitions of war of all kinds must be furnished, or the war must end in defeat and disgrace. This is not the time for any lover of his country to inquire as to the state of the money market, or ask whether he can so invest his surplus capital as to yield him a large return. No return, and no profit, can be desirable, if followed by national dissolution, or national disgrace. Present profit, thus acquired, is but the precursor of future and speedy destruction. No investment can be so surely profitable as that which tends to insure the national existence.

I am encouraged in the belief that by the recent legislation of Congress our finances may soon be placed upon a sounder and more stable footing. The present deranged condition of the currency is imputable, in a great degree, to disturbances arising from the withdrawal of necessary checks, often inevitable in time of war, when expenditures must largely exceed any possible supply of coin. The opportunities thus presented to acquire sudden wealth have led to vicious speculation, a consequent increase in prices and violent fluctuation. The remedy is to be found only in controlling the necessity which begets the evil. Hitherto we have felt the need of more extensive and vigorous taxation. Severe comment has been made upon what seemed to many an undue timidity and tardiness of action, on the part of Congress, in this regard. I deem it but just to say that very great misapprehension has existed, and perhaps still exists, upon this point. Legislators, like all others, have much to learn in a new condition of affairs. An entirely new system was to be devised, and that system must necessarily be the growth of time and experience. It is not strange that first efforts should have proved imperfect and inadequate. To lay heavy burdens on a great and patriotic people in such a manner as to be equal, and as to occasion the least amount of suffering or annoyance, requires time and caution, and vast labor; and, with all these, experience is needful to test the value of the system, and correct its errors. Such has been the work which Congress was called upon to perform. I am happy to say, that daily results are proving the Internal Revenue Act to exceed in efficiency the most sanguine expectations of its authors. In the month of June, 1863, it yielded about four and one-half millions of dollars, while the corresponding month of this year returned about fifteen millions under the same law. Under the new law, which went into operation on the first day of the present month, the Treasury not unfrequently receives one million in a day. As time and experience enable the officers employed in collecting the revenue to enforce the stringent provisions of the new law, I trust that a million per day will be found the rule and not the exception. Still much space is undoubtedly left for improvement in the law, and in its administration, as a greater amount of necessary information is acquired. The proper sources of revenue, and the most effective modes of obtaining it, are best developed in the execution of existing laws. And I have caused measures to be initiated which will, it is believed, enable Congress so to improve and enlarge the system as, when taken in connection with the revenue from customs, and other sources, to afford an ample and secure basis for the national credit. Only on such a basis, and in a steady and vigorous restraint upon currency, can a remedy be found for existing evils. Such restraint can only be exercised when the government is furnished with means to provide for its necessities. But without the aid of a patriotic people, any government is powerless, for this or any other desirable end.

The denominations of the notes proposed to be issued, ranging from fifty to five thousand dollars, place these securities within the reach of all who are disposed to aid their country. For their redemption the faith, honor and prosperity of that country are solemnly pledged. A successful issue to this contest, now believed to be near at hand, will largely enhance their value to the holder; and peace once restored, all burdens can be lightly borne. He who selfishly withholds his aid in the hope of turning his available means to greater immediate profit, is speculating upon his country's misfortunes, and may find that what seems to be present gain leads only to future loss. I appeal, therefore, with confidence to a loyal and patriotic people, and invoke the efforts of all who love their country, and desire for it a glorious future, to aid their government in sustaining its credit, and placing that credit upon a stable foundation.

W. P. FESSENDEN,
Secretary of the Treasury.

A BANK LIBRARY.

1. Manual for Notaries Public and Bankers, June, 1864, 1 vol. 8vo.,.... $3 00
2. The Bankers' Common Place Book, by GILBART, MCCULLOCH, &c.,. 1 25
3. STORY on the Law of Promissory Notes, Guaranties, &c.,........ 6 00
4. STORY on the Law of Bills of Exchange, Foreign and Inland,...... 6 00
5. KENT's Commentaries on American Law, ninth edition, 4 vols.,.... 20 00
6. The Banking System of the State of N.Y., &c., by JOHN CLEAVELAND, 4 00
7. A Treatise on the Law of Bankers and Banking, by JAMES GRANT,. 3 50
8. The Laws of Business for Business Men, by Professor PARSONS,... 3 50
9. CHITTY on the Law of Bills of Exchange, Promissory Notes, &c.,... 5 00
10. The Cyclopedia of Commerce, one vol. 8vo., 2,000 pp., 2d edition, 8 00
11. The Merchants and Bankers' Register, 1852—1864, 13 vols.,...... 13 00
12. The Bankers' Magazine and Statistical Register, 9 vols., 1856—1864, 54 00
13. The Banks and Clearing-House of New-York, by J. S. GIBBONS,... 2 00
14. Digest of the Laws of the United States to 1862,............,..... 8 00
15. The Ways and Means of Payment, by S. COLWELL,............ 3 00
16. Historical and Statistical Account of Foreign Commerce U. S.,.... 2 00
17. History of the Bank of England, (published 1863,) enlarged,...... 3 50
18. PARSONS on Promissory Notes and Bills of Exchange, (1863,)..... 12 00
19. GILBART on Banking, (new edition,) Revised by I. S. HOMANS, 8vo., 2 50
20. Sixteen Decisions of the Supreme Court of U. S. on Taxation of
    Government Bonds, &c.,................................ 1 00
21. All the Acts of Congress relating to Loans and Currency, 1842–1864, 1 25
22. Hand-Book of U. S. Tax Law; with Decisions, Notes, &c.,...... 1 25
23. Chronicles and Characters of the Stock Exchange, by FRANCIS,.... 1 25
24. System of Bank Book-keeping, by C. C. MARSH, enlarged ed., 1864, 7 00
25. The Merchants and Bankers' Almanac for 1863 and 1864, each.... 1 25
26. History of Banking in Europe, by WM. J. LAWSON, 1 vol. 8vo.,.... 2 50
27. The National Bank Act of 1864, 1 vol., with List of Banks,...... 1 25
28. Popular Lectures on Commercial Law, for the use of Merchants and
    Business Men, by Judge SHARSWOOD,..................... 1 00
29. The Funding System of the U. S. and Great Britain, 8vo.,......... 8 00
30. DELISSER's Interest Tables at Seven Per Cent., 4to.,............ 3 00
31. EDWARDS on the Law of Bills of Exchange and Notes,........... 6 00
32. BYLES on the Law of Bills of Exchange, Banks, &c.,............ 5 50

☞ Ten per cent. extra will be charged for copies prepaid by mail.

THE BANKERS' MAGAZINE AND STATISTICAL REGISTER,

PUBLISHED MONTHLY, FIVE DOLLARS PER ANNUM. Contains—

1. A monthly List of New Banks established in the United States.
2. A monthly List of New National Banks. Location, President, Cashier, and Capital of each.
3. A monthly List of New Banking Firms established in the several States.
4. Lowest and Highest Prices, monthly, of leading Government, State, Rail-Road, Coal and
   other Stocks.
5. Daily Price of Gold at the New-York Stock Exchange.
6. Monthly List of New Appointments of Presidents and Cashiers of Banks.
7. Decisions in reference to Bills of Exchange, Promissory Notes, Banks, Bonds, Insurance,
   Usury, &c.
8. Monthly Review of the Money Market and Stock Market of New-York.
9. Monthly Report of Banking operations abroad.
10. New Banking Laws of the State of New-York and of other States.
11. Forms (prepared by N. Y. bank counsel) of Bank Bonds for Bank Officers.
12. Banking Statistics of every State in the Union, and of England, France, &c.

I. S. HOMANS, Jr., 46 Pine-street, N. Y.

HISTORY

OF

THE BANK OF ENGLAND,

ITS TIMES AND TRADITIONS,

From 1694 to 1844.

BY JOHN FRANCIS.

FIRST AMERICAN EDITION, WITH NOTES, ADDITIONS AND AN APPENDIX, INCLUDING STATISTICS OF
THE BANK TO THE CLOSE OF THE YEAR 1861,

BY I. SMITH HOMANS.

New-York:

PUBLISHED AT THE OFFICE OF THE BANKERS' MAGAZINE,

Chamber of Commerce and Underwriters' Building, Nos. 61 & 63 William St.

1862.

FRAUDS ON BANKS AND BANKERS.

THE BANKERS' MAGAZINE for September, 1854, contains, *entire*, the noted case of ELLIS & MORTON *vs.* THE OHIO LIFE INSURANCE AND TRUST COMPANY, with the decision of the SUPERIOR COURT OF CINCINNATI, as delivered by JUDGE STORER, revised by him, and furnished for publication in the Bankers' Magazine. Also, a summary of all the cases (forty in number) referred to by the Court, from the English and American reports; these have now been brought together for the first time, and form a valuable series of cases for the Banker, upon the subject of Fraudulent Bills, Bank Checks, Bank Notes.

SUMMARY OF CASES.

ENGLISH CASES.—1. *Young* vs. *Grote* ; 2. *Snow* vs. *Peacock* ; 3. *Beckwith* vs. *Corrall* ; 4. *Slater* vs. *West* , 5. *Arbouin* vs. *Anderson* ; 6. *Goodman* vs. *Harvey* ; 7. *Uther* vs. *Rich* ; 8. *Foster* vs. *Pearson* ; 9. *Bramah* vs. *Roberts* ; 10. *Price* vs. *Neal* ; 11. *Wilkinson* vs. *Lutwidge* ; 12. *Jenyns* vs. *Fowler* ; 13. *Bass* vs. *Clive* ; 14. *Smith* vs. *Mercer* ; 15. *Jones* vs. *Ryde* ; 16. *Bruce* vs. *Bruce* ; 17. *Smith* vs. *Chester* ; 18. *Lickbarrow* vs. *Mason* ; 19. *Wilkinson* vs. *Johnson* ; 20. *Cook* vs. *Masterman* ; 21. *Gill* vs. *Cubitt* ; 22. *Down* vs. *Halling* ; 23. *Hall* vs. *Fuller* ; 24. *Lawson* vs. *Weston* ; 25. *Crook* vs. *Jadis* ; 26. *Backhouse* vs. *Harrison*.

AMERICAN CASES.—1. *Levy* vs. *Bank U. S.* ; 2. *Bank U. S.* vs. *Bank State of Georgia* ; 3. *Gloucester Bank* vs. *Salem Bank* ; 4. *Bank of St. Albans* vs. *Farmers' and Mechanics' Bank* ; 5. *Bank of Commerce* vs. *Union Bank, N. Y.* ; 6. *Goddard* vs. *Merchants' Bank* ; 7. *Marsh* vs. *Small* ; 8. *City Bank, N. O.,* vs. *Girard Bank* ; 9. *Herf & Co.,* vs. *Schultz* ; 10. *Powell* vs. *Jones* ; 11. *Talbot* vs. *Bank of Rochester* ; 12. *Canal Bank* vs. *Bank of Albany* ; 13. *Cone* vs. *Baldwin* ; 14. *Wheeler* vs. *Guild* ; 15. *Adams* vs. *Otterback* ; 16. *Weisser* vs. *North River Bank, N. Y.*

Every Bank and Private Banker, Bank Officer and Bank Director should have a copy of these decisions.

The present volume of the Bankers' Magazine will contain a History of Banking in Tennessee, Kentucky, Indiana, Illinois, Louisiana, and other States; an alphabetical list of cashiers in the United States; a list of private bankers in every town and city of the United States.

Monthly, Five Dollars per annum. All orders to be addressed

J. SMITH HOMANS, 70 Wall Street, N. Y.

From a Massachusetts Cashier.—I read your work with great interest, and I know that I have profited by it. I am confident that my success is owing in a great measure to the information which your pages have given me.

I consider your work a very valuable one, and highly deserving the support of bankers, and of the business community. You have my best wishes for your success.
April, 1851.   J. D. PLUMB, *Cashier,* Albany.

Your periodical is one of the most valuable of the day.
April, 1851.   J. S. GIBBONS, *Cashier Ocean Bank, N. Y.*

                                                          Agricultural Bank, Herkimer, N. Y.
We prize the work very highly, and are very desirous of having it complete, that it may be bound and preserved. The information it contains on the subjects of banking and finance is invaluable to the banker, the merchant, and the financier.
September, 1850.

I am surprised to learn that there are so many banks in our State not on your subscription list. Now I might almost add my amazement that there should be a solitary one, of sound character, not eagerly availing itself of a work so useful and valuable as I regard your Magazine. It will give me pleasure to promote its circulation by any means in my power.

I heard it very highly spoken of in London when there recently, and especially so by Mr. Gilbart, whose praise in that respect is worth having.
April, 1851.   WATTS SHERMAN, *Cashier, Albany City Bank.*

Foreign and Domestic Commerce, Rail-Roads, Canals, Steam, &c.

PUBLISHED SEPTEMBER, 1859.

A NEW AND REVISED EDITION OF THE

Cyclopedia of Commerce

AND COMMERCIAL NAVIGATION,

By J. SMITH HOMANS, Secretary of the Chamber of Commerce; and J. SMITH HOMANS, Jr.,
author of "An Historical and Statistical Sketch of the Foreign Commerce of the U. S."

One Volume, 8vo., 2,000 pp., strongly bound in muslin,.... $6
Two Volumes, 8vo., sheep, 2,000 pp.,.................. $8

The first edition of the CYCLOPEDIA OF COMMERCE having been exhausted, and a favorable estimate placed upon the work by the public, we have deemed it important that in the second edition, recent commercial changes should be noticed, and that leading statistics of the United States and of leading countries throughout the world should be added.

The Editors have taken pains to introduce a few fresh subjects, and to substitute new tabular details of recent date, for the pages contained in the first edition. The following articles have been either introduced, re-written or enlarged:

Average. Average Bond.

Bahia, Trade of. Baltimore, Trade of; Banks of, 1857–'59. Bank of France, Operations of 1857–'59. Banks of the United States, for years 1858–'59. Banks (Savings) of Great Britain, United States and France. Bankruptcy in 1858, Statistics of. Belgium, Commerce, Tariff, Port Regulations, etc., of. Board of Trade, History of. Books, Copyright Law of Europe and United States. Boston, Commercial Statistics of, 1858. Breadstuffs, Statistics of, 1857–'58. Buffalo, Trade of, 1858.

Cadiz, Trade of, 1857. Canada, Finances, Revenue, Debt and Trade of, 1857–'58. China, Recent Treaties with. Carpets, Manufacture and Statistics of. Carriages, Manufacture and Statistics of. Charleston, South Carolina, Commerce of, 1850–'58. Chili. Clearing-House, Statistics of, 1856–'58. Coal and Coal Trade of Great Britain and United States. Coffee and Coffee Trade, 1857–'58. Cotton Crop, 1856–'58. Cotton Consumption and Distribution throughout the World. Cuba, Commerce and Finances of, 1857–'58.

Denmark, Commerce and Trade of, 1857–'58. Elsineur.

France, Commerce, Debt and Finances of, 1857–'58.

Genoa, Commerce, Harbor, etc., of. Germany, Commerce, Manufactures, etc., of. Glass, Statistics of, 1857–'58. Great Britain, Commerce, Manufactures and other Statistics of, 1857–'58. Imports and Exports of each year, 1801–'59.

Hamburg, Commerce of, 1856–'59. Hanse Towns, Commerce of, 1856–'58. Hides, Imports and Exports of, 1858. Hospitals. Hospital System of the United States.

Ice. Ice Trade. Insurance (Life), Statistics of.

Jamaica, Commerce and Statistics of. Key West, Commerce and Wreckers of.

Lace, Manufacture and Statistics of. Leipsic, Liberia, Products and Commerce of. Lloyd's, Sketch of; Instructions to Agents of. Louisiana, Statistics of, 1857–'58.

Madeira. Mahogany, Production and Uses of, for Ships, etc. Malta, Population, Commerce and recent Statistics of. Manufactures of the United States. Marseilles, Trade, etc., of, 1857–'58.

Netherlands, Commerce of. Newfoundland. New-Granada. New-York State, Commerce, Trade, Manufacture and Banks, 1858. New-York City, Debt, Population and Property, 1857–'58.

Paraguay, Commercial Relations of. Philadelphia, Commerce, Manufactures, etc., of, 1857–'58. Philippine Islands. Porto Rico, Providence, Commerce, Manufactures, etc., of, 1857–'58.

Quebec, Commerce, Trade and Shipping of. Russia, Commerce, Trade and Shipping of.

St. Christopher, Revenue and Commerce of. San Domingo, Revenue and Commerce of. San Salvador, Revenue and Commerce of. Sardinia, Revenue and Commerce of. Shipping, Suggestions by the Merchants and Underwriters of New-York. Sierra Leone, Palm Oil and other Trade of. Stadt Dues. Sugar, Product, Consumption and Price of, each year, 1815–1858.

Tahiti, Whaling Trade, etc., of. Tea, Crop, Consumption and Price of, each year, 1801–'58. Treaties, Commercial, with all Nations. Trieste, Commerce, Tonnage and Trade of.

United States, Commerce, Banks and Shipping of.

Whaling, Whale Trade, History and Statistics of. Wool, Crop, Exports and Imports of every Country, each year, 1840–'58. Wrecks. Wreckers. Rules of Wrecking.

Zoll-Verein, Manufactures and Trade of, 1857–'58.

The Navy Department, by order dated July, 1859, has directed that the "Cyclopedia of Commerce" be added to the list of books furnished for the use of Vessels and Navy Yards of the United States.

LIST OF MAPS AND ENGRAVINGS IN THE CYCLOPEDIA OF COMMERCE.

Chart of New-York Bay and Harbor. Artesian Wells. Atlantic Ocean. Harbor of Bahia. Harbor of Cape Town. Harbor of Constantinople. Dry Docks. Harbor of Elsineur. Straits of Gibraltar. Gulf Stream. Marine Dynamometer. Heights of Waves. Harbor and City of Havana. Life Boats. Light Houses. Harbor of Rio Janeiro.

The Cyclopedia of Commerce.—"This valuable work has entirely superseded the use of McCulloch's Dictionary of Commerce. In addition to the valuable portions of Mr. McCulloch's work, contained in the "Cyclopedia of Commerce," the latter contains very copious information in reference to the great staples of the United States, and of the world at large; the Commerce of the several States, &c., brought down to the year 1859. The Cyclopedia is now, by order of the Navy Department, adopted as the text-book for the naval service of the United States. The new and revised edition of 1859 is particularly acceptable to our commercial and nautical men, and is an essential work to every counting room and to every merchant ship."—*N. Y. Courier & Enquirer.*

Copies, either bound in one volume, 2,000 pages, price $6; or in two volumes, 1,000 pages each, $8, may be had of

J. S. HOMANS,

Office Bankers' Magazine,   N. Y

FOR THE CASHIER'S DESK.

MANUAL FOR NOTARIES PUBLIC AND BANKERS,

NEW EDITION—1863.

A MANUAL FOR THE USE OF NOTARIES PUBLIC AND BANKERS, COMPRISING A SUMMARY OF THE LAW OF BILLS OF EXCHANGE AND PROMISSORY NOTES—BOTH IN EUROPE AND THE UNITED STATES. CHECKS ON BANKERS AND SIGHT BILLS, WITH APPROVED FORMS OF PROTEST AND NOTICE OF PROTEST, AND REFERENCES TO IMPORTANT LEGAL DECISIONS. ADAPTED TO THE USE OF NOTARIES PUBLIC AND BANK OFFICERS. By BERNARD ROELKER, OF THE NEW-YORK BAR. New edition, with extensive additions.

By J. SMITH HOMANS, Editor of "The Bankers' Magazine," and Notary Public.

This edition contains the following new subjects, with all the new cases in the United States and Great Britain, in reference to the Law of Bills of Exchange, Promissory Notes, Protests, &c.:

CHAPTER I.—OF BILLS OF EXCHANGE—1. *What is a Bill?* 2. *Bills and Notes Accepted and Made by Agents.* 3. *Time of Presentment.* 4. *Excuses for Due Presentment.* 5. *Parol Acceptance.* 6. *Destruction of a Bill.* 7. *Statutes as to Acceptance.* 8. *Acceptance of a Non-existing Bill.* 9. *Erasure of an Acceptance.* 10. *Waiver of Acceptance.* 11. *Conditional Acceptance.* 12. *Rights of an Acceptor, Supra Protest.* 13. *What is a Promissory Note?* 14. *Notes Payable to a Fictitious Person.* 15. *Where is the Place of Payment?* 16. *Bank Checks.* 17. *Days of Grace on Sight Bills.* 18. *Circumstances to Excuse Presentment.* 19. *Presentment—by whom to be made.* 20 *Mode of Presentment.* 21. *Mode of Demand.* 22. *Exceptions to Demand.* 23. *Waiver of Protest.* 24. *Protest of Foreign Bills.* 25. *Lex Loci.* 26. *Notices to Endorsers in the same Town.* 27. *When Notice to be Given.* 28. *Notice to Non-residents.* 29. *An Endorser Bound to Give Notice.* 30. *Notice by Special Messenger.* 31. *Notice to Joint Endorsers.* 32. *Death of Endorser.* 33. *Acceptor, Supra Protest.* 34. *To what Place should Notice be Sent?* 35. *Decisions in New-York.* 36. *Persons by whom Notice is Given.* 37. *Agents.*
CHAPTER II.—38. *The Liability of Banks as Agents.* 39. *Can a Demand be made legally by a Notary's Clerk?* 40. *Form of Notice.* 41. *Use of Printed Signatures.* 42. *Excuses for want of Presentment.* 43. *Waiver of Notice.* 44. *Guaranty of Bills.* 45. *Lost Bills.* 46. *Forged Bills and Notes.* 47. *Days of Grace on Checks.*
CHAPTER III.—OF THE TRANSFER OF BILLS AND NOTES.—I. WHO MAY TRANSFER.—1. *Transfers by Infants.* 2. *Transfers by Married Women.* 3. *Transfers by Executors, Assignees, Trustees, Partners, &c.* II. To WHOM THE TRANSFER MAY BE MADE.—*Transfers to prior Endorsers.* III. MODES OF TRANSFER.—1. *Transfers of Non-Negotiable Bills or Notes.* 2. *Transfers of Negotiable Bills or Notes.* 3. *Transfer of Bills, &c., payable to a fictitious person.* 4. *Assignment of Negotiable Bills.* 5. *Effect of Omission to Endorse.* 6. *Form of Endorsement.* 7. *Form of Endorsement by Agent.* 8. *Kinds of Endorsement.* 9. *Blank Endorsement.* 10. *Endorsements in full and partly in full.* 11. *Restrictive Endorsements.* 12. *Qualified Endorsements.* 13. *Conditional Endorsements.* IV. TIME OF TRANSFER.—1. *Effect of Transfer before maturity.* 2. *Endorsements upon Blank Paper.* V. OBLIGATIONS OF ENDORSERS.—1. *Obligations upon Transfer by Endorsement.* 2. *Obligations upon Transfer by Delivery.* 3. *Revocation of Endorsement.*
CHAPTER IV.—OF LETTERS OF CREDIT.
CHAPTER V.—OF BANK NOTES.—*Forgery. Liability for Redemption of Stolen Bills.*
CHAPTER VI.—*The Laws of each State in reference to Interest and Damage on Bills of Exchange.*

APPENDIX FOR 1863.

Decisions of the Supreme Court, U. S., and of every State in the Union, in the years 1860, 1861 *and part of* 1862, *in cases of Banking, Bills of Exchange, Promissory Notes, Usury, &c.*

One volume, octavo, pp. 360, Price $3 00. (Copies bound in muslin will be mailed to order, price Three Dollars, including postage, pre-paid.)

J. SMITH HOMANS, Editor of the Bankers' Magazine,

63 WILLIAM STREET, *New-York City.*

Manual for Bankers.—The title of this book, which we transcribe at length above, indicates with sufficient distinctness its nature and objects. Though we possess in general the professional dislike to Manuals and other Short-Hand Methods of cramming law into laymen, which "enterprising Publishers" occasionally inflict on society, we must except from the rules of condemnation this accurate and convenient little treatise, both on account of its subjects and its manner of preparation. A work of the kind is continually needed by that class to which it addresses itself. From the character of their business they must frequently be called upon to solve, in action, questions upon the loss of bills and notes, which even a well-read lawyer would hesitate to answer off-hand. This being so, the Notary Public, who very rarely has had any legal training, must need at his elbow some safe guide to which he can turn with confidence in an emergency for the requisite information. Such we can state from examination, is the work before us. It is a compact and careful summary of the law on subjects which it treats, with a collection of the Statistics and Notes of the principal Decisions bearing thereon. A resume of the Law of the Continent of Europe, with regard to bills and notes, is prefixed, and will be found of very considerable value.—*American Law Magazine.*

From such examination as I have been enabled to give your "Manual for Notaries Public," I am of opinion that it is convenient and highly useful aid to Bank Officers and Notaries, very many of whom are unskilled in the forms and not versed in the legal questions which are so important and of frequent occurrence in the discharge of their duties. J. B. TEMPLE, *Cashier Farmers' Bank of Ky.*

Your "Manual for Notaries Public," from the partial examination given, we take pleasure in saying, is the most satisfactory and concise work of the kind we have ever examined, and we think it admirably adapted to the purposes intended; not only convenient to the Banker and non-professional man, but a work we think calculated to save great labor and investigation of the more ponderous works on that subject, to the legal profession. TUCKER, BRANNIN & Co., *Bankers, Louisville, Ky.*

4.

THE

NATIONAL BANKS

OF THE

UNITED STATES.

~~~~~~~~~~~~~~~~

AN ACT TO PROVIDE A NATIONAL CURRENCY, SECURED
BY A PLEDGE OF UNITED STATES BONDS, AND
TO PROVIDE FOR THE CIRCULATION
AND REDEMPTION THEREOF.
APPROVED JUNE 3, 1864.

———————

WITH

A SYNOPSIS OF EACH SECTION ; AN ALPHABETICAL INDEX, AND A LIST
OF NATIONAL BANKS IN OPERATION JUNE, 1864.

═══════════

New-York :

PUBLISHED AT THE OFFICE OF THE BANKERS' MAGAZINE,
No. 46 Pine Street, Corner of William Street,
(COMMERCIAL ADVERTISER BUILDING.)

June, 1864.—Price One Dollar.

A BANK LIBRARY.

☞ Ten per cent. extra will be charged for copies prepaid by mail.

THE BANKERS' MAGAZINE AND STATISTICAL REGISTER,

PUBLISHED MONTHLY, FIVE DOLLARS PER ANNUM. Contains—

1. A monthly List of New Banks established in the United States.
2. A monthly List of New National Banks. Location, President, Cashier, and Capital of each.
3. A monthly List of New Banking Firms established in the several States.
4. Lowest and Highest Prices, monthly, of leading Government, State, Rail-Road, Coal and
   other Stocks.
5. Daily Price of Gold at the New-York Stock Exchange.
6. Monthly List of New Appointments of Presidents and Cashiers of Banks.
7. Decisions in reference to Bills of Exchange, Promissory Notes, Banks, Bonds, Insurance,
   Usury, &c.
8. Monthly Review of the Money Market and Stock Market of New-York.
9. Monthly Report of Banking operations abroad.
10. New Banking Laws of the State of New-York and of other States.
11. Forms (prepared by N. Y. bank counsel) of Bank Bonds for Bank Officers.
12. Banking Statistics of every State in the Union, and of England, France, &c.

I. S. HOMANS, Jr., 46 Pine-street, N. Y.

IMPORTANT FINANCIAL DOCUMENTS,
Published in the Bankers' Magazine and Statistical Register,

[The official organ of the American Geographical and Statistical Society] for the year 1862.

· THE

BANKERS' COMMON PLACE BOOK.

PRICE, $1.25.

200 *pp. Duodecimo, containing :*

I. A Treatise on Banking. By A. B. JOHNSON, Esq., President Ontario Bank, Utica.
II. Ten Minutes' Advice on Keeping a Banker. By J. W. GILBART, Esq., of the London and Westminster Bank.
III. BYLES on the Law of Bills of Exchange and Promissory Notes.
IV. Remarks on Bills of Exchange. By J. RAMSAY M'CULLOCH, Esq.
V. Forms of Bills of Exchange, in eight European Languages.
VI. Forms of Notice of Protest of Bills and Notes, with Remarks.
VII. Synopsis of the Bank Laws of Massachusetts, in force January, 1851.
VIII. Decisions of the Supreme Judicial Court of Massachusetts, in reference to Banking.
IX. On the Duties, Omissions and Misdoings of Bank Directors. By A. B. JOHNSON, Esq., of Utica.
X. A Prize Essay on Banking. "Suggestions to Young Cashiers, on the Duties of their Profession." By LORENZO SABINE. [*This Essay obtained the premium of one hundred dollars, offered by the editor of the Bankers' Magazine, for the best contribution on the subject.*]
XI. A Numismatic Dictionary, or List of all the Coins known in all Ages.

"Many excellent works on Banking, and a still greater number of articles on Banking, in magazines and other periodical publications, have appeared in America. We have before us one of no common merit. It is entitled A Treatise on Banking—The Duties of a Banker, and his personal requisites therefor. By A. B. JOHNSON, President of the Ontario Branch Bank, at Utica, in the State of New York. The first part—'The Bank'—contains a clear exposition of some important principles of Banking and Currency, and a comparison between the Safety Fund System and the Free Bank system established in New York. The second part—'The Banker'—is of a highly practical character ; and it shows that however widely the banks of England and of America may differ in their principles, the fields of their operations, their constitutions and their privileges, yet the practical operations, the qualifications of their bankers, the dangers to which they are exposed, and the means necessary to success, are much the same in both countries."—*London Bankers' Magazine.*

Persons who reside at a distance can receive the work per mail, postage paid, to any part of the United States. Price $1.25.

New York:

PUBLISHED AT THE OFFICE OF THE BANKERS' MAGAZINE,

No. 162 PEARL-STREET.

Published June, 1864.   Price Three Dollars.

A

MANUAL

FOR THE USE OF

NOTARIES PUBLIC

AND

BANKERS;

COMPRISING A SUMMARY OF THE LAW OF BILLS OF EXCHANGE AND OF PROMISSORY NOTES, BOTH
IN EUROPE AND THE UNITED STATES—CHECKS ON BANKERS—AND SIGHT BILLS—WITH
APPROVED FORMS OF PROTEST AND NOTICE OF PROTEST; AND REFERENCES
TO IMPORTANT LEGAL DECISIONS; ESPECIALLY ADAPTED FOR
THE USE OF NOTARIES PUBLIC AND BANKERS.

By BERNARD ROELKER, A. M., OF THE NEW-YORK BAR.

FOURTH EDITION.

WITH NUMEROUS ADDITIONS IN REFERENCE TO BILLS OF EXCHANGE AND PROMISSORY NOTES;
PROTEST; TRANSFER OF BILLS AND NOTES; LETTERS OF CREDIT; FORGED BILLS; FRAUDULENT
AND LOST BANK BILLS; SIGHT BILLS, &C., AND REFERENCES TO RECENT DECISIONS
IN THE UNITED STATES AND ENGLISH COURTS; AND A SYNOPSIS OF THE USURY
LAWS OF EACH STATE, AND THE LAW OF DAMAGES ON PROTESTED BILLS.

By I. SMITH HOMANS,

Editor of the "Bankers' Magazine and Statistical Register," New-York.

New-York:

PUBLISHED AT THE OFFICE OF THE BANKERS' MAGAZINE.
—
1864.

THE

LOAN, REVENUE AND CURRENCY

ACTS OF 1863.

~~~~~~~~~~~~~~~~

NEW-YORK:

PUBLISHED AT THE OFFICE OF

THE BANKERS' MAGAZINE AND STATISTICAL REGISTER,

63 William Street, corner of Cedar Street.

March, 1863.—Price One Dollar.

THE

BANKERS' MAGAZINE,

AND

Statistical Register.

EDITED BY I. SMITH HOMANS.

"No expectation of forbearance or indulgence should be encouraged. Favor and benevolence are not the attributes of good banking. Strict justice and the rigid performance of contracts are its proper foundation."
"The Revenue of the State is THE STATE; in effect, all depend upon it, whether for support or for reformation."

VOLUME EIGHTEENTH,

OR,

VOLUME THIRTEENTH, NEW SERIES,

FROM JULY, 1863, TO JUNE, 1864, INCLUSIVE.

NEW-YORK:

PUBLISHED BY I. SMITH HOMANS, JR.,
No. 46 PINE ST., CORNER OF WILLIAM ST., COMMERCIAL ADVERTISER BUILDING.

1863—'64.

GENERAL INDEX

TO THE

EIGHTEENTH VOLUME (OR THIRTEENTH VOLUME, NEW SERIES)

OF THE

Bankers' Magazine and Statistical Register

FROM

JULY, 1863, TO JUNE, 1864, BOTH INCLUSIVE.

☞ Complete copies of the present volume can be supplied by the publisher, to order. Price, in numbers, $5; or substantially bound, $6. Separate Nos. will be furnished to subscribers to order, for the completion of their volumes, at subscription price. Bound copies will be supplied in exchange for the Nos. All orders to be addressed, by mail, to I. SMITH HOMANS, Jr., No. 46 Pine-street, corner of William-street, Commercial Advertiser Building, New-York.

BOOKS FOR THE CASHIER'S DESK.

I. Manual for Notaries Public and Bankers. New Edition will be ready April, 1864. A Manual for the use of Notaries Public and Bankers, comprising a summary of the Law of Bills of Exchange and Promissory Notes, both in Europe and the United States, Checks on Bankers and Sight Bills, with approved forms of Protest and Notice of Protest, and references to important legal decisions. Adapted to the use of Notaries Public and Bank Officers. By BERNARD ROELKER, of the New-York Bar. New edition, with extensive additions. By J. SMITH HOMANS, late Editor of "The Bankers' Magazine," and Notary Public. This edition contains many subjects, with all the new cases in the United States and Great Britain, in reference to the Law of Bills of Exchange, Promissory Notes, Protests, &c.; with the decisions of the Supreme Court, U. S., and of every State in the Union, in the years 1860, 1861 and part of 1862, in cases of Banking, Bills of Exchange, Promissory Notes, Usury, &c. One volume, octavo, pp. 350. Price $3 00. (Copies bound in muslin will be mailed to order, price $3.00, including postage, prepaid.)

II. Marsh's Bank Book-keeping. The Theory and Practice of Book-keeping and Joint-Stock Accounts, Exemplified and Elucidated in a Complete Set of Account Books. Printed in colors, arranged in accordance with the Principles of Double Entry, and embracing the Routine of Business, from the Organization of a Company to the Declaration of a Dividend, with all the Forms and Details, and an Original Diagram. By C. C. MARSH.

*** This is the only work published in this country or in Europe, exemplifying Book-keeping in Banks and Joint-Stock Companies. Second edition. 1 vol., 4to., 292 pages. Bound and gilt; published in the best style. $7. $7.75 per mail. A glance at the title-page of this work will show the reader that it is unique. Nothing of the kind has hitherto been made the subject of a separate treatise. To those who require the book, this specialty is its chief recommendation. They will obtain here exactly what they require and nothing else. It is encumbered with no extraneous matter.

III. Principles of Political Economy. Applied to Banking, the Currency and the Usury Laws. Principles of Political Economy, with some of their applications to Social Philosophy. By JOHN STUART MILL. From the Fifth London Edition. Two volumes, octavo. Price $6. Among the subjects treated of by Mr. MILL in these volumes, demanding the consideration of Bankers and Capitalists, may be enumerated the following: Money, as Dependent on Demand and Supply, and on Cost of Production—Of a Double Standard and Subsidiary Coins—Of Credit as a Substitute for Money—Influence of Credit on Prices—Of an Inconvertible Paper Currency—Of Excess of Supply—Of a Measure of Value—Of International Trade—International Values—Of Foreign Exchanges—Distribution of the Precious Metals—Influence of Currency on the Exchanges—Of the Rate of Interest—A Convertible Paper Currency—Influence of the Progress of Society on Production and Distribution—Of the Influence of Government—Taxation—National Debt—Capital—Labor—Property—Wages—Exchange, &c. Guided by such a work, and making it the basis of instruction in a science so intimately connected with the every day duties of the citizen, there will be little danger of our people in the next generation yielding to low and sordid views on any of the great questions connected with our civil or national economy. The habit will be formed of referring all such questions to foundation principles, instead of apparent party or temporary policy. We cannot, therefore, but expect great good to follow the extensive circulation of this masterly work.

IV. The Banks and the Clearing House of New-York. By J. S. GIBBONS.

*** A Description of the Clearing House, with diagram. A new edition will be ready in April, 1864. Price $2.00.

V. Bryant and Stratton's Commercial Law for Business Men; including Bankers, Merchants, Farmers, Mechanics, &c. Adapted to all the States of the Union, with a variety of Practical Forms. By AMOS DEAN, LL. D., Professor of Law in the Law Department of the University of Albany. One volume, octavo, pp. 550. $3.50, (or $4 per mail.) Copies of the above works supplied to order by the publisher of the Bankers' Magazine, New-York.

Cyclopedia of Commercial and Business Anecdotes. Will be ready soon. A collection, original and selected, of the choicest, most striking, and *recherché* anecdotes of Merchants, Traders, Bankers, Mercantile celebrities, Millionaires, Bargain Makers, &c., and comprises interesting reminiscences and facts, remarkable traits and humors, with notable sayings, dealings, experiences and witticisms. The work will be illustrated with forty steel portraits of noted Merchants of Europe, Asia and America, as well as wood-cuts of amusing incidents in their lives, and views of many business localities. The work will be published in two large volumes, octavo, over 400 pages each. Price $6.00.

A Manual for Notaries Public and Bankers.

I. *A Manual for the use of Notaries Public and Bankers.* One vol. 8 vo. By B. ROELKER, *Esq. Published at the Office of the* BANKERS' MAGAZINE, *New-York.* pp. 360. Price, $3.00.

THE fourth edition of this work is now issued, under the supervision of the Editor of the BANKERS' MAGAZINE. The additions now made to the original work comprise the decisions of the last eight years, in the Supreme Court of the United States, and in the several States, in reference to Banking, Bills of Exchange, Promissory Notes, Usury, &c. There is no other law work extant, embracing such a variety of subjects as the present, important both to the banker and the notary public. Among these matters we may enumerate: I. A Summary of the Laws of each State in the Union in reference to the Rates of Interest, Penalties for Usury, and the Damages on Protested Bills of Exchange. II. The Law of Letters of Credit. III. Fraud and Fraudulent Bills. IV. Forged Checks. V. Transfer of Bills and Notes. VI. Obligations of Endorsers. VII. New forms of Protest and Notice of Protest. VIII. Forms of Bills of Exchange in Eight European Languages, &c.

The "Manual" is thus, from its numerous and reliable authorities, domestic and foreign, rendered a valuable aid to the banker and to the notary. In fact it may, with advantage, be placed in the hands of the bank clerk who wishes to make progress in his profession.—*New-York Commercial Advertiser, July,* 1864.

MANUAL FOR BANKERS.—The title of this book, which we transcribe at length above, indicates with sufficient distinctness its nature and objects. Though we possess in general the professional dislike to Manuals and other Short-Handed Methods of cramming law into laymen, which "Enterprising Publishers" occasionally inflict on society, we must except from the rules of condemnation this accurate and convenient little treatise, both on account of its subjects and its manner of preparation. A work of this kind is continually needed by the class to which it addresses itself. From the character of their business they must frequently be called upon to solve, in action, questions upon the loss of bills and notes, which even a well read lawyer would hesitate to answer off-hand. This being so, the notary public, who very rarely has had any legal training, must need at his elbow some safe guide to which he can turn with confidence in an emergency for the requisite information. Such we can state, from examination, is the work before us. It is a compact and careful summary of the law on subjects which it treats, with a collection of the statistics and notes of the principal decisions bearing thereon. A resumé of the law of the Continent of Europe, with regard to bills and notes, is prefixed, and will be found of very considerable value.—*American Law Magazine.*

From such examination as I have been enabled to give your "Manual for Notaries Public," I am of opinion that it is a convenient and highly useful aid to bank officers and notaries, very many of whom are unskilled in the forms, and not versed in the legal questions which are so important and of frequent occurrence in the discharge of their duties. J. B. TEMPLE, *Cashier Farmers' Bank of Kentucky.*

Your "Manual for Notaries Public," from the partial examination given, we take pleasure in saying, is the most satisfactory and concise work of the kind we have ever examined, and we think it admirably adapted to the purposes intended; not only convenient to the banker and non-professional man, but a work we think calculated to save great labor and investigation of the more ponderous works on that subject, to the legal profession.

TUCKER, BRANNIN & Co., *Bankers, Louisville, Kentucky.*

II. *The National Bank Act of 1864.*

THE publisher of the BANKERS' MAGAZINE, New-York, has issued, in one volume octavo, (*price, one dollar,*) THE NATIONAL BANK ACT OF JUNE, 1864; to which are added—I. An Analysis of each Section. II. A copious Alphabetical Index to Subjects in the Act. III. A List of all the National Banks in Operation, June, 1864; the Names of President and Cashier of each, Capital, &c. IV. Blank leaves for Memoranda.

VALUABLE DOCUMENTS FOR BANKERS,

Bank Directors, Bank Clerks, Merchants, Insurance Companies, &c,

CONTAINED IN THE BANKERS' MAGAZINE, 1863-4.

1. List of National Banks in the United States, location and County, names of President and Cashier of each, present and limited capital of each. (*Published monthly.*)

2. Annual Report of the Superintendent of the Bank Department of the State of New-York, 1863 and 1864.

3. The Product of Gold and Silver throughout the World in 1846 and 1863. Tabular Statement of the Supply in every Country.

4. The National Banking Law of 1863. 1. Letter from the Comptroller of the Currency. 2. Regulations adopted as to the establishment of Banks under the Law. 3. Payment of the Five-Twenty Bonds.

5. List of Banks in the U. S. Location, Name of President and Cashier, and Capital of each.

6. Fifteen important Decisions of the Supreme Court of the United States, in reference to the Taxation of Government Securities by States and Cities.

7. Lowest and Highest Prices of Stocks, each month, 1861-1864. (*Monthly.*)

8. Internal Revenue Decisions. 1. Drafts drawn by Bankers. 2. Tax on Circulation and Deposits. 3. Purchase and Sale of Gold and Silver.

9. The Daily Price of Gold at New-York, 1862-1864. (*Published monthly.*)

10. Historical sketch of Banking and Repudiation in Mississippi.

11. Banks of the City of New-York. Surplus Profits and Price of Stock of each.

12. Decision of the Supreme Court of New-York on Legal Tender Notes.

13. Decision of the Court of Appeals of New-York on Legal Tender Notes.

14. Annual Report of the Société Générale du Credit Mobilier.

15. The Usury Laws and the National Banking System. By HIRAM KETCHUM, Jr., Esq., of New-York.

16. European Banking and Finance. 1. Finances of France. 2. Oriental Tea Company. 3. Vienna Bank. 4. The Consolidated Bank. 5. New Mining Company. 6. Bank of Brazil. 7. New-Zealand Banking. 8. Financial Association, London and Paris. 9. Belgian Bank. 10. Austrian Loan of 1863. 11. Petroleum in England.

17. Recent Frauds on Bankers. 1. Wolverhampton, England. 2. Robbery at Warsaw. 3. United States Greenbacks. 4. Reward for Honesty.

18. New Banking Laws of the State of New-York. 1. Bank Directors. 2. Taxation of Bank Capital. 3. Stocks for Circulation. 4. Savings Banks. 5. To enforce the Responsibility of Stockholders. 6. The Manhattan Company. 7. Payment of State Interest in Coin. 8. Act to prevent Frauds in Stamps. 9. To limit the number of Notaries Public.

19 Legal Miscellany—Redemption of Bank Notes—Legal Tender in Small Coins—Case of the Bank of the State of Missouri.

20 State and City Finances—Michigan, Virginia, Louisiana, Ohio, Pittsburgh, Philadelphia, Cincinnati, &c.

21. Answers of the Comptroller of the Currency to questions in relation to the National Currency Act.

22. Trial and conviction of HIDES and LIGHT, for the Forgery of Treasury Notes, before the Crown Court.

23. Report of the Joint Committee of the Clearing Houses of New-York, Boston and Philadelphia, on the Tax Law of the United States.

24. On the Debt and Resources of the United States. By Dr. WM. ELDER.

25. Memoirs of Remarkable Misers of the Nineteenth Century.

26. Decisions of all the State Courts, 1860-62, on Banking, Bills, Notes, Usury, &c.

27. Finances of the Revolution. Letter of JOHN JAY on Public Credit and Loans, and Finance.

28. English views of Banking. The Theory and Practice of Banking, with the Elementary Principles of Currency, Prices, Credit and Exchanges. By HENRY DUNNING McLEOD.

NEW-YORK:

PUBLISHED MONTHLY BY J. SMITH HOMANS, Jr.

CHAMBER OF COMMERCE AND UNDERWRITERS' BUILDING, Nos. 61 AND 63 WILLIAM STREET.

Terms, Five Dollars Per Annum.

IMPORTANT BANKING DOCUMENTS

FOR THE USE OF

BANK OFFICERS, DIRECTORS, PRIVATE BANKERS, &c.

Contained in the new Volume of the Bankers' Magazine, July, 1859—June, 1860.

Copies of the Volume supplied to order, in Numbers, $5, or substantially bound, $5 75.

I. A SOUND CURRENCY.—What is it? Hints concerning the evils that result from falsification of the Currency. By John H. Hunt. Read before the New-York Board of Currency.

II. THE MORALS OF TRADE.—1. Bank Directors and Stockholders. 2. Fraudulent Bills of Exchange. 3. Over Trading. 4. Adulteration of Food. 5. Causes of Fraud. 6. Remedies Proposed. (*From the Westminster Review, April,* 1859.)

III. THE CHIEF METALS OF THE WORLD.—1. Copper. 2. Tin. 3. Lead. 4. Gold. 5. Silver. 6. Platina. 7. Zinc and Antimony. 8. Mercury. 9. Arsenic. 10. Gems. 11. Pewter.

IV. REMARKS ON THE PRESENT CURRENCY SYSTEM.—Prepared for publication during the Panic of 1857, and read, by request, before the Currency Reform Association of New-York, July 6, 1859. By Mr. Peter Cooper.

V. THE FUTURE VALUE OF GOLD.—1. Money, a medium of exchange. 2. Conditions which determine the value of money. 3. Effect of new discoveries. 4. Difference between coin and bullion. 5. Influences which prevent a diminution in value. 6. Consequences of a diminution in value. 7. Case of the English fundholders.

VI. NEW-YORK CITY BANKS.—Capital, circulation, profits, deposits, bank balances, loans, stocks, bonds and mortgages, real estate, cash items, specie of each, June 30.

VII. CURRENCY, BANKING AND CREDIT.—By James S. Ropes, Esq., of Boston.

VIII. ANNUAL REPORT ON THE NEW-YORK ASSAY OFFICE.—Coins of the United States—Fluctuations in Prices—California Trade.

IX. SAVINGS BANKS.—Comparative table of deposits in the City and State of New-York, for each year. 1856, 1857, 1858, 1859.

X. FRAUDS ON LIFE INSURANCE COMPANIES.—The great French Insurance Frauds.

XI. BANK FINANCIERING IN PENNSYLVANIA.—Frauds on the Monongahela Valley Bank.

XII. GOLD, SILVER AND FREE TRADE—With Statistics of Product of Gold and Silver in all countries of the World, 1849—1859.

XIII. RATES OF FOREIGN EXCHANGE, each week, January, 1855, to December, 1858.

XIV. FOREIGN BANK STATISTICS.—1. Bank of France. 2. Bank of England. 3. National Bank of Greece.

XV. LEGAL MISCELLANY.—Bank Checks—Failure—Liability of Banks—Deposited checks need not be presented for payment the day of their deposit.

XVI. THE PROGRESS OF BANKING IN GREAT BRITAIN.—The Bank Act of 1844—Failures of 1857—Loans to Bill Brokers—Forced issue of £2,000,000 Bank Notes—Bank Failures in Scotland—Crisis in Ireland—Crisis in Liverpool—Continental Banks—Price of Gold—Opinions of Lord Overstone—Yearly average of Notes, 1844—1859—Evidence of Messrs. Neave, Sampson, Lloyd, Rodwell, &c.—Failures of Commercial Houses—Joint Stock Banks—Fluctuations in Prices.

XVII. BANKING IN SCOTLAND. [London Times.]

XVIII. ON MONETARY PANICS.—Correspondence between the Hon. Amasa Walker, of Massachusetts, and Homer Stansfield, Esq., of Burley, England.

XIX. PLANTERS' BANK BONDS OF MISSISSIPPI.—Message of the Governor, 1859.

XX. HISTORY OF TRIBUNALS OF COMMERCE OF FRANCE, HAMBURGH, &c.

XXI. ROBERT MORRIS, THE FINANCIER.—Statement of the Financial Affairs of the United States from February, 1781, to September, 1789, accompanied with a statement of the tax assessed on, and of the amount paid by, each State, under the resolution of Congress in 1781, 1782—from April, 1782, to September, 1789. By Michael Nourse, Esq., of Washington; with a biographical sketch of Mr. Morris, by J. M. Sanderson, Esq.

XXII. ATTACHMENT LAWS AND STATUTES OF LIMITATION in the several States and Territories.

XXIII. A SKETCH OF THE HISTORY OF BANKING IN TENNESSEE.

XXIV. THE VALIDITY OF COUNTY, TOWN AND CITY BONDS issued to Rail-Road Corporations, with the Interest Laws of the State of Illinois.

XXV. ALPHABETICAL LIST of sixteen hundred Cashiers in the United States, January, 1860.

XXVI. ANNUAL REPORT of the Superintendent of the Banking Department of New-York, January, 1860.

XXVII. THE BANKS OF CANADA, January, 1860; their Managers, Cashiers and Foreign Agents; Capital, Liabilities, &c., of each Bank.

XXVIII. THE BANKING SYSTEM OF NEW-YORK.—Review of the Annual Report of the Bank Department for the year 1859.

XXIX. THE HIGHEST AND LOWEST PRICES of English Consols, Railway Shares, &c., each month, 1859.

XXX. COMMERCE AND CURRENCY OF THE UNITED STATES. (*From the North American Review, for January,* 1860.)

XXXI. ANNUAL REPORT of the New-England Association for the Suppression of Counterfeiting.

XXXII. ANNUAL REPORT of the Director of the Mint on the Coinage of the U. S. January, 1860.

XXXIII. AN EXAMINATION OF THE THEORY and the effect of Laws regulating the amount of Specie in Banks. By Samuel Hooper, of Boston.

☞ Copies of the above volume may be had in numbers, price $5; or substantially bound in calf backs, $5 50; or morocco extra, $5 75.

J. SMITH HOMANS, Jr., PUBLISHER BANKERS' MAGAZINE,
New-York.

A Manual for Notaries Public and Bankers.

I. *A Manual for the use of Notaries Public and Bankers.* One vol. 8 vo. By B. ROELKER, *Esq. Published at the Office of the* BANKERS' MAGAZINE, *New-York.* pp. 360. Price, $3.00.

THE fourth edition of this work is now issued, under the supervision of the Editor of the BANKERS' MAGAZINE. The additions now made to the original work comprise the decisions of the last eight years, in the Supreme Court of the United States, and in the several States, in reference to Banking, Bills of Exchange, Promissory Notes, Usury, &c. There is no other law work extant embracing such a variety of subjects as the present, important both to the banker and the notary public. Among these matters we may enumerate: I. A Summary of the Laws of each State in the Union in reference to the Rates of Interest, Penalties for Usury, and the Damages on Protested Bills of Exchange. II. The Law of Letters of Credit. III. Fraud and Fraudulent Bills. IV. Forged Checks. V. Transfer of Bills and Notes. VI. Obligations of Endorsers. VII. New forms of Protest and Notice of Protest. VIII. Forms of Bills of Exchange in Eight European Languages, &c.

The "Manual" is thus, from its numerous and reliable authorities, domestic and foreign, rendered a valuable aid to the banker and to the notary. In fact it may, with advantage, be placed in the hands of the bank clerk who wishes to make progress in his profession.—*New-York Commercial Advertiser, July,* 1864.

MANUAL FOR BANKERS.—The title of this book, which we transcribe at length above, indicates with sufficient distinctness its nature and objects. Though we possess in general the professional dislike to Manuals and other Short-Handed Methods of cramming law into laymen, which "Enterprising Publishers" occasionally inflict on society, we must except from the rules of condemnation this accurate and convenient little treatise, both on account of its subjects and its manner of preparation. A work of this kind is continually needed by the class to which it addresses itself. From the character of their business they must frequently be called upon to solve, in action, questions upon the loss of bills and notes, which even a well read lawyer would hesitate to answer off-hand. This being so, the notary public, who very rarely has had any legal training, must need at his elbow some safe guide to which he can turn with confidence in an emergency for the requisite information. Such we can state, from examination, is the work before us. It is a compact and careful summary of the law on subjects which it treats, with a collection of the statistics and notes of the principal decisions bearing thereon. A resumé of the law of the Continent of Europe, with regard to bills and notes, is prefixed, and will be found of very considerable value.—*American Law Magazine.*

From such examination as I have been enabled to give your "Manual for Notaries Public," I am of opinion that it is a convenient and highly useful aid to bank officers and notaries, very many of whom are unskilled in the forms, and not versed in the legal questions which are so important and of frequent occurrence in the discharge of their duties. J. B. TEMPLE, *Cashier Farmers' Bank of Kentucky.*

Your "Manual for Notaries Public," from the partial examination given, we take pleasure in saying, is the most satisfactory and concise work of the kind we have ever examined, and we think it admirably adapted to the purposes intended; not only convenient to the banker and non-professional man, but a work we think calculated to save great labor and investigation of the more ponderous works on that subject, to the legal profession.

TUCKER, BRANNIN & Co., *Bankers, Louisville, Kentucky.*

II. *The National Bank Act of* 1864.

THE publisher of the BANKERS' MAGAZINE, New-York, has issued, in one volume octavo, (*price, one dollar,*) THE NATIONAL BANK ACT OF JUNE, 1864; to which are added—I. An Analysis of each Section. II. A copious Alphabetical Index to Subjects in the Act. III. A List of all the National Banks in Operation, June, 1864; the Names of President and Cashier of each, Capital, &c. IV. Blank leaves for Memoranda.

BOOKS FOR THE CASHIER'S DESK.

I. Manual for Notaries Public and Bankers. New Edition will be ready April, 1864. A Manual for the use of Notaries Public and Bankers, comprising a summary of the Law of Bills of Exchange and Promissory Notes, both in Europe and the United States, Checks on Bankers and Sight Bills, with approved forms of Protest and Notice of Protest, and references to important legal decisions. Adapted to the use of Notaries Public and Bank Officers. By BERNARD ROELKER, of the New-York Bar. New edition, with extensive additions. By J. SMITH HOMANS, late Editor of "The Bankers' Magazine," and Notary Public. This edition contains many subjects, with all the new cases in the United States and Great Britain, in reference to the Law of Bills of Exchange, Promissory Notes, Protests, &c.; with the decisions of the Supreme Court, U. S., and of every State in the Union, in the years 1860, 1861 and part of 1862, in cases of Banking, Bills of Exchange, Promissory Notes, Usury, &c. One volume, octavo, pp. 350. Price $3 00. (Copies bound in muslin will be mailed to order, price $3.00, including postage, prepaid.)

II. Marsh's Bank Book-keeping. The Theory and Practice of Book-keeping and Joint-Stock Accounts, Exemplified and Elucidated in a Complete Set of Account Books. Printed in colors, arranged in accordance with the Principles of Double Entry, and embracing the Routine of Business, from the Organization of a Company to the Declaration of a Dividend, with all the Forms and Details, and an Original Diagram. By C. C. MARSH.

** This is the only work published in this country or in Europe, exemplifying Book-keeping in Banks and Joint-Stock Companies. Second edition. 1 vol., 4to., 292 pages. Bound and gilt, published in the best style. $7. $7.75 per mail. A glance at the title-page of this work will show the reader that it is unique. Nothing of the kind has hitherto been made the subject of a separate treatise. To those who require the book, this specialty is its chief recommendation. They will obtain here exactly what they require and nothing else. It is encumbered with no extraneous matter.

III. Principles of Political Economy. Applied to Banking, the Currency and the Usury Laws. Principles of Political Economy, with some of their applications to Social Philosophy. By JOHN STUART MILL. From the Fifth London Edition. Two volumes, octavo. Price $6. Among the subjects treated of by Mr. MILL in these volumes, demanding the consideration of Bankers and Capitalists, may be enumerated the following : Money, as Dependent on Demand and Supply, and on Cost of Production—Of a Double Standard and Subsidiary Coins—Of Credit as a Substitute for Money—Influence of Credit on Prices—Of an Inconvertible Paper Currency—Of Excess of Supply—Of a Measure of Value—Of International Trade—International Values—Of Foreign Exchanges—Distribution of the Precious Metals—Influence of Currency on the Exchanges—Of the Rate of Interest—A Convertible Paper Currency—Influence of the Progress of Society on Production and Distribution—Of the Influence of Government—Taxation—National Debt—Capital—Labor—Property—Wages—Exchange, &c. Guided by such a work, and making it the basis of instruction in a science so intimately connected with the every day duties of the citizen, there will be little danger of our people in the next generation yielding to low and sordid views on any of the great questions connected with our civil or national economy. The habit will be formed of referring all such questions to foundation principles, instead of apparent party or temporary policy. We cannot, therefore, but expect great good to follow the extensive circulation of this masterly work.

IV. The Banks and the Clearing House of New-York. By J. S. GIBBONS.

** A Description of the Clearing House, with diagram. A new edition will be ready in April, 1864. Price $2.00.

V. Bryant and Stratton's Commercial Law for Business Men ; including Bankers, Merchants, Farmers, Mechanics, &c. Adapted to all the States of the Union, with a variety of Practical Forms. By AMOS DEAN, LL. D., Professor of Law in the Law Department of the University of Albany. One volume, octavo, pp. 550. $3.50, (or $4 per mail.) Copies of the above works supplied to order by the publisher of the Bankers' Magazine, New-York.

Cyclopedia of Commercial and Business Anecdotes. Will be ready soon. A collection, original and selected, of the choicest, most striking, and *recherché* anecdotes of Merchants, Traders, Bankers, Mercantile celebrities, Millionaires, Bargain Makers, &c., and comprises interesting reminiscences and facts, remarkable traits and humors, with notable sayings, dealings, experiences and witticisms. The work will be illustrated with forty steel portraits of noted Merchants of Europe, Asia and America, as well as wood-cuts of amusing incidents in their lives, and views of many business localities. The work will be published in two large volumes, octavo, over 400 pages each. Price $6.00.

VALUABLE DOCUMENTS FOR BANKERS,

Bank Directors, Bank Clerks, Merchants, Insurance Companies, &c.

CONTAINED IN THE BANKERS' MAGAZINE, 1863-4.

1. List of National Banks in the United States, location and County, names of President and Cashier of each, present and limited capital of each. (*Published monthly.*)

2. Annual Report of the Superintendent of the Bank Department of the State of New-York, 1863 and 1864.

3. The Product of Gold and Silver throughout the World in 1846 and 1863. Tabular Statement of the Supply in every Country.

4. The National Banking Law of 1863. 1. Letter from the Comptroller of the Currency. 2. Regulations adopted as to the establishment of Banks under the Law. 3. Payment of the Five-Twenty Bonds.

5. List of Banks in the U. S. Location, Name of President and Cashier, and Capital of each.

6. Fifteen important Decisions of the Supreme Court of the United States, in reference to the Taxation of Government Securities by States and Cities.

7. Lowest and Highest Prices of Stocks, each month, 1861-1864. (*Monthly.*)

8. Internal Revenue Decisions. 1. Drafts drawn by Bankers. 2. Tax on Circulation and Deposits. 3. Purchase and Sale of Gold and Silver.

9. The Daily Price of Gold at New-York, 1862-1864. (*Published monthly.*)

10. Historical sketch of Banking and Repudiation in Mississippi.

11. Banks of the City of New-York. Surplus Profits and Price of Stock of each.

12. Decision of the Supreme Court of New-York on Legal Tender Notes.

13. Decision of the Court of Appeals of New-York on Legal Tender Notes.

14. Annual Report of the Société Générale du Credit Mobilier.

15. The Usury Laws and the National Banking System. By Hiram Ketchum, Jr., Esq., of New-York.

16. European Banking and Finance. 1. Finances of France. 2. Oriental Tea Company. 3. Vienna Bank. 4. The Consolidated Bank. 5. New Mining Company. 6. Bank of Brazil. 7. New-Zealand Banking. 8. Financial Association, London and Paris. 9. Belgian Bank. 10. Austrian Loan of 1863. 11. Petroleum in England.

17. Recent Frauds on Bankers. 1. Wolverhampton, England. 2. Robbery at Warsaw. 3. United States Greenbacks. 4. Reward for Honesty.

18. New Banking Laws of the State of New-York. 1. Bank Directors. 2. Taxation of Bank Capital. 3. Stocks for Circulation. 4. Savings Banks. 5. To enforce the Responsibility of Stockholders. 6. The Manhattan Company. 7. Payment of State Interest in Coin. 8. Act to prevent Frauds in Stamps. 9. To limit the number of Notaries Public.

19. Legal Miscellany—Redemption of Bank Notes—Legal Tender in Small Coins—Case of the Bank of the State of Missouri.

20. State and City Finances—Michigan, Virginia, Louisiana, Ohio, Pittsburgh, Philadelphia, Cincinnati, &c.

21. Answers of the Comptroller of the Currency to questions in relation to the National Currency Act.

22. Trial and conviction of Hides and Light, for the Forgery of Treasury Notes, before the Crown Court.

23. Report of the Joint Committee of the Clearing Houses of New-York, Boston and Philadelphia, on the Tax Law of the United States.

24. On the Debt and Resources of the United States. By Dr. Wm. Elder.

25. Memoirs of Remarkable Misers of the Nineteenth Century.

26. Decisions of all the State Courts, 1860-62, on Banking, Bills, Notes, Usury, &c.

27. Finances of the Revolution. Letter of John Jay on Public Credit and Loans, and Finance.

28. English views of Banking. The Theory and Practice of Banking, with the Elementary Principles of Currency, Prices, Credit and Exchanges. By Henry Dunning McLeod.

⁕ This is the only Magazine published in the United States containing Bank Statistics of the several States—Names of New Banks established, and New Banking firms—Daily Price of Gold, and quotations of Bank, Rail-Road, State and other Stocks.

☞ Each volume of the Bankers' Magazine and Statistical Register commences in July and ends in June following, making an annual volume of 1,000 pages octavo.

NEW-YORK:

PUBLISHED MONTHLY BY J. SMITH HOMANS, Jr.

CHAMBER OF COMMERCE AND UNDERWRITERS' BUILDING, Nos. 61 AND 63 WILLIAM STREET.

Terms, Five Dollars Per Annum.

IMPORTANT TO BANKS, BANK OFFICERS, PRIVATE BANKERS AND CAPITALISTS.

I. Sixteen Decisions of the Supreme Court of the United States, in reference to Taxation of U. S. Loans by States and Cities. One volume octavo. Price $1.

This volume includes the celebrated cases of "McCulloh vs. State of Maryland," "Weston vs. City of Charleston," &c.

II. Acts of Congress relating to Loans and the Currency. From 1842 to March, 1863, inclusive. Price $1.

This volume includes the Loan Act of 1863, ($900,000,000,) and others essential to a correct understanding of the United States Bonds.

III. The Bank and Revenue Acts of 1863. One volume octavo. $1.

This volume includes—1. An Act to Provide Ways and Means for the Support of the Government to June, 1864.—Approved March 8, 1863. With a copious index. II. An Act Amendatory of the Internal Revenue Laws, and for other purposes.—Approved March 8, 1863. III. An Act to Provide a National Currency, secured by a Pledge of United States Stocks, and to provide for the Circulation and Redemption thereof.—Approved February 25, 1863. With marginal notes and an index.

IV. A Manual for Notaries Public and Bankers—Containing a History of Bills of Exchange; Forms of Protest and Notices of Protest; the Laws of each State in reference to Protest, Interest, Damages on Bills, &c.; the decisions of 1858—1863, upon Bills, Notes, Protest, &c. 1 vol. octavo. $3.

V. The Cyclopedia of Commerce and Commercial Navigation, with twenty-three engravings and Maps. A complete exhibit of the Finances and Commerce, Manufactures and Trade of all Nations. Edited by J. Smith Homans and J. Smith Homans, Jr. Octavo, 2,000 pp. $8.

VI. Historical and Statistical Account of the Foreign Commerce of the United States and of each State, for each year, 1820—1856; the Exports to, and Imports from, every Foreign Country each year, 1820—1856; Commerce of the Early Colonies; Origin and Early History of each State. 8vo., pp. 200. $1.50.

VII. The Merchants and Bankers' Almanac for 1863, containing valuable documents for Bankers. Price $1.25.

VIII. The Merchants and Bankers' Almanac for 1864, containing complete lists of Banks, National Banks, Private Bankers, Savings Banks, &c., Banking and Coinage Statistics, &c. One volume octavo. Price $1.25. (Free by mail.)

IX. The History of the Bank of England; its Times and Traditions. By John Francis. First American edition, with notes, additions, and an appendix, including Statistics of the Bank to the close of the year 1861. By J. Smith Homans. One volume octavo, pp. 476. Price $3.

X. Chronicles and Characters of the London Stock Exchange. By John Francis, author of "The History of the Bank of England." One vol. 8vo. $1.50.

The American Edition has copious Tables of Stocks, 1694—1847.

XI. A Practical Treatise on Banking. By James W. Gilbart, Esq. Second American edition, with additions. By J. Smith Homans. One vol. 8vo., pp. 553. $2.50.

XII. The History of Banking, with a comprehensive account of the Origin, Rise and Progress of the Banks of England, Scotland and Ireland. By William John Lawson. Revised, with notes on the History of Banking in America. By J. Smith Homans. 1 vol. 8vo., pp. 346. $2.

XIII. The Bankers' Common Place Book. By Gilbart, A. B. Johnson, Sabine, McCulloch, &c. $1. With a Numismatic Dictionary, Prize Essay for Cashiers, &c.

XIV. The Bankers' Magazine and Statistical Register, five dollars per annum.

This is the only work published in this country that gives complete banking and financial statistics of the States—the latest decisions on Bills, Notes, Banking, &c.

☞ Every Bank and Bank: should have a copy of the Bankers' Magazine, (substantially bound at the end of the year,) for reference by the Directors, Officers and Clerks. It contains the only report of the progress of Banking in the several States—New Bank Laws—New Bank Cases—Foreign Banking—Financial Statistics—Fluctuations in Stocks and in Gold, &c.

TERMS FIVE DOLLARS PER ANNUM. NEW-YORK: PUBLISHED MONTHLY BY

J. SMITH HOMANS, Jr.

Notice to Private Bankers.—The Bankers' Magazine, monthly, and the Bankers' Almanac, annually, furnish the best medium to Bankers for advertising. These works circulate in every State in the Union, in Europe, South America, &c.

RATES FOR BANKERS' CARDS.

In Bankers' Magazine, one-fifth of a page, one year, [including subscription,]	$20 00
In Bankers' Almanac, one-fifth of a page, one year,	15 00
In Bankers' Magazine and Almanac, one-fifth of a page, one year,	25 00
Bankers' Magazine and Statistical Register, subscription, one year,	5 00
Bankers' Almanac, 1864, [including postage],	1 25

www.ingramcontent.com/pod-product-compliance
Lightning Source LLC
Chambersburg PA
CBHW030614270326
41927CB00007B/1180